THE MINOR P...
Volume 2

Ed Landry

Habakkuk
Zephaniah
Joel
Nahum

Uplifting Christian Books
Nashville, Tennessee 2020

The Minor Prophets - Volume 2
Teaching and Preaching from the Often Neglected Books of the Bible
#2 in the easy-to-understand Bible Commentary series on the Minor Prophets
Copyright © 2020 by Uplifting Christian Books

Published in Nashville, TN by Uplifting Christian Books
All rights reserved.

Printed in the Philippines by SAM Printing Press, Cebu City
Printed in the USA by Kindle Direct Publishing

Author - Ed Landry
Special thanks to our dedicated editorial team - Marcia P., Tom and Janet T., Herb M., Mitzi C., Ora Lee K., Dell W., Janet L., Lyndell M., Roy and Linda M., Carol S., and Mike and Elaine F.

Book and cover design by Ed and Janet Landry.
Illustrations by Ed Landry.
Special thanks to The Bible Project for several small illustrations.
Additional Development team - The Thursday Group

ISBN-13: 978-0-9990931-4-6

Printed in the United States of America.

Dedicated

To all the Pastors and Teachers of God's amazing
Word. My hope is that these three volumes will
inspire you to communicate the timeless messages
found in the 12 minor prophets. The minor
prophets are often neglected in pulpits and
classrooms. My prayer is that these easy-to-read
books will help bring them back to the people.

Ed Landry
Missionary, First Love International Ministries

Some free recommended resources to help in your studies

The Blue Letter Bible

This is a free App (BLB) for your phones which has a wide spectrum of Bible study tools. To use on your computers and laptops, go to:
https://www.blueletterbible.org/

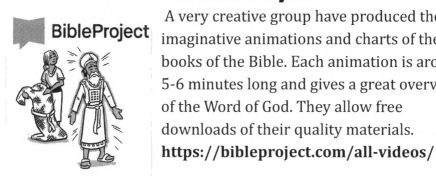

The Bible Project

A very creative group have produced these imaginative animations and charts of the books of the Bible. Each animation is around 5-6 minutes long and gives a great overview of the Word of God. They allow free downloads of their quality materials.
https://bibleproject.com/all-videos/

Precept Austin

A massive commentary and Bible resource website. The site contains word by word commentary of the entire Bible with some 20,000 resources. This site is for serious Bible students. One of the best organized and helpful sites on the INTERNET. It will take a while to learn to navigate the site but worth the effort.
https://www.preceptaustin.org/

Got Questions

This online resource contains over 600,000 Bible questions and answers. Their leadership and staff represent some of the finest evangelical Bible colleges and seminaries in the USA. Comprehensive, yet concise.
https://www.gotquestions.org/

Bible.Org

A large collection of Bible commentaries and expostions arranged by topic, book, verse, words, etc. The site also has the NET Bible (2nd edition) with its 58,000+ notes, Greek, Hebrew, texts linked to Strongs numbers. It allows you to search all the translations of the Bible to find your favorite verses. The commentary section uses the works of hundreds of top theologians and evangelical authors. Find it at:
https://bible.org/

Bible Hub

A huge collecton of word studies, commentaries, Bible versions. Type in a verse and then choose what you want and you will have more resources than you can imagine. Like any web site, it will take a little time to understand it and take advantage of its power.
https://biblehub.com/

HABAKKUK

Habakkuk and God have a conversation about His plan to use the Babylonians to discipline His people, Judah!

"Look among the nations! Observe! Be astonished! Wonder! Because I am doing something in your days— You would not believe if you were told."

Habakkuk 1:5

Introduction

Who was Habakkuk?

The book of Habakkuk contains the oracle seen by this prophet (Habakkuk 1:1, also 3:1). That is officially all that is stated about Habakkuk. He was a prophet. The various predictions he makes in his three-chapter book help us date the book between 640-609 B.C. He lived as a prophet during the reigns of Josiah and Jehoiakim. He prophesied before the Babylonian invasion in 586 B.C. Habakkuk would have lived at the end of Josiah's reign and the beginning of Jehoiakim's. He was contemporary with Jeremiah and Zephaniah who also prophesied just before the Babylonian invasion.

Habakkuk 2:4 ("The just shall live by faith") was quoted in two New Testament books, Romans 1:17 and Galatians 3:11. It is also paraphrased in Hebrews 10:38. This alone gives credibility to the book of Habakkuk. He was a prophet and the book is inspired work. Habakkuk's name means "He who clings." His name will be very meaningful in this story. He and God have a strong discussion about the evil in the land and the judgment that is coming. In the end, Habakkuk will have to be satisfied clinging to God, hanging on tight, when things don't make sense. It is a story of struggle and faith, teaching us to to trust God when we don't know what to do.

The uniqueness of Habakkuk.

Habakkuk lived in Judah, the Southern Kingdom, even though he does not mention Judah in his book. The Northern Kingdom had been overthrown by Assyria. A unique thing about the book is that it is a record of a conversation between God and Habakkuk. Each speaks and responds and this continues. This question and answer format began with a discussion about the discipline method God would use with His wayward people. Habakkuk almost argued with God, telling God that He can't do what He planned. It is fascinating to watch the grace of God in action. God never got angry with His prophet, yet He made sure Habakkuk, like Job, realized God is God and He does everything well even when we don't understand His ways.

Also unique is that Habakkuk is one of three prophets of God who prophesied against nations other than Israel and Judah. The others are Nahum who addressed Assyria, Habakkuk addressed Babylon and Obadiah delivered a judgment against Edom.

Habakkuk dealt with a unique question as well. How can a holy and just God discipline Judah by using wicked people as His instrument of correction? God will answer that question and in the end, Habakkuk will realize there are some things we can't fully understand. The just man must learn to have faith in God because He is God.

Summary

"Habakkuk's prophecy was directed to a world that, through the eyes of God's people, must have seemed on the edge of disaster. Even when the Northern Kingdom had been destroyed in 722 B.C., God's people remained in Judah. However, with another powerful foreign army on the rampage, faithful people like Habakkuk were wondering what God was doing. Hadn't He given the land to His people? Would He now take it away? Habakkuk's prayer of faith for the remainder of God's people in the face of such destruction still stands today as a remarkable witness of true faith and undying hope." (Chuck Swindoll)

Habakkuk main sections

- Habakkuk introduces himself. (1:1)
- Habakkuk's first complaint: Why does the evil in the land go unpunished? (1:2–4)
- God's answer: it will be punished. The Babylonians will do it. (1:5–11)
- Habakkuk's second complaint: How can a just God use wicked Babylon to punish people more righteous than themselves? (1:12—2:1)
- God's answer: All the unrighteous will be punished, Judah, and ultimately Babylon as well. God will honor those who trust Him, faith will be rewarded. (2:2–20)
- Habakkuk's prayer: After asking for manifestations of God's wrath and mercy (as he has seen in the past), he closes with a confession of trust and joy in God. (3:1-19)

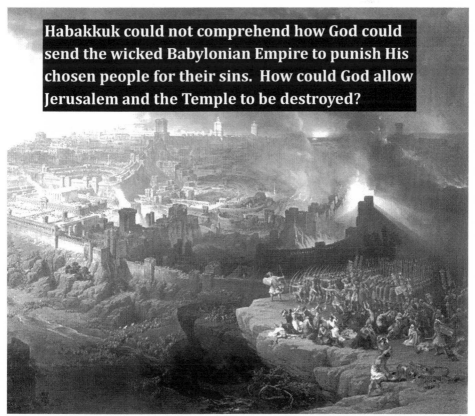

Habakkuk could not comprehend how God could send the wicked Babylonian Empire to punish His chosen people for their sins. How could God allow Jerusalem and the Temple to be destroyed?

Habakkuk One

Habakkuk cries out to God about the sin of his people (1:1-4).

[1] The oracle which Habakkuk the prophet saw.
[2] How long, O LORD, will I call for help,
And You will not hear?
I cry out to You, "Violence!"
Yet You do not save.
[3] Why do You make me see iniquity,
And cause *me* to look on wickedness?
Yes, destruction and violence are before me;
Strife exists and contention arises.
[4] Therefore the law is ignored
And justice is never upheld.
For the wicked surround the righteous;
Therefore justice comes out perverted.

Habakkuk, like many of the prophets, had a strong sense of justice. He believed evil needed to be punished. He struggled with the fact that sin was all around him, in his homeland, but heaven seemed silent. God was doing nothing, so he thought. Why was God taking so long?

> "The oracle which Habakkuk the prophet saw.
> How long, O Lord, will I call for help,
> And You will not hear?" (1:1, 2)

Habakkuk must have been a man of God who had a very sensitive heart. He hated to see the violence in the land and it bothered him to see sinful actions and attitudes. Every time he turned around, he witnessed something disgusting to him. He saw his people fighting and squabbling instead of being thankful and rejoicing. Habakkuk even blamed God that he was being forced to see those things. He felt helpless to stop it.

> **"I cry out to You, "Violence!"**
> **Yet You do not save.**
> **Why do You make me see iniquity,**
> **And cause me to look on wickedness?**
> **Yes, destruction and violence are before me;**
> **Strife exists and contention arises."** (1:2.3)

Habakkuk was in conflict and torment. He wanted God to act. The Law of God which Habakkuk respected was ignored by the leaders of the land. Because of that, evil was not punished, justice was never dispensed. The wicked ran freely since they were not held accountable for their sins.

> **"Therefore the law is ignored**
> **And justice is never upheld.**
> **For the wicked surround the righteous;**
> **Therefore justice comes out perverted."** (1:4)

God's surprising answer to Habakkuk's cry for help (1:5-11).

5 "Look among the nations! Observe!
Be astonished! Wonder!
Because *I am* doing something in your days—
You would not believe if you were told.
6 "For behold, I am raising up the Chaldeans,
That fierce and impetuous people
Who march throughout the earth
To seize dwelling places which are not theirs.
7 "They are dreaded and feared;
Their justice and authority originate with themselves.
8 "Their horses are swifter than leopards
And keener than wolves in the evening.

Their horsemen come galloping,
Their horsemen come from afar;
They fly like an eagle swooping *down* to devour.
9 "All of them come for violence.
Their horde of faces *moves* forward.
They collect captives like sand.
10 "They mock at kings
And rulers are a laughing matter to them.
They laugh at every fortress
And heap up rubble to capture it.
11 "Then they will sweep through *like* the wind and pass on.
But they will be held guilty,
They whose strength is their god."

God certainly introduced His answer to Habakkuk's questions with appropriate words.

> **"Look among the nations! Observe!**
> **Be astonished! Wonder!**
> **Because I am doing something in your days—**
> **You would not believe if you were told."** (1:5)

Brace yourself, Habakkuk! What you are about to hear will be beyond anything you could imagine. God's ways have been described as "mysterious." To Habakkuk, God's answer to his questions will be much more than mysterious; it will seem contradictory to His nature. He is holy and righteous, so Habakkuk expected his answer to reflect that. God even told Habakkuk he would not believe God would do such a thing.

What was it that God was going to do?

> **"For behold, I am raising up the Chaldeans,**
> **That fierce and impetuous people**
> **Who march throughout the earth**
> **To seize dwelling places which are not theirs."** (1:6)

God was going to use the fierce, pagan, Babylon Empire, to be His instrument to discipline Judah, the apple of God's eye, His cherished chosen people. Habakkuk, as God had just said, could not believe it. Yes, Judah had sinned and became unfaithful to God, but to use a nation like Babylon (the Chaldeans) for punishment, made no sense to the prophet.

God was fully aware of the wicked Chaldeans (Babylonians) and described them to His dumbfounded prophet in verses 6-11. Here is what we learn from God's description of that enemy people:

- God was taking responsibility for sending the army. He is the ultimate King of all nations and He is Sovereign over the affairs of men (1:6).
- They were a fierce army, terrible and dreadful (1:6, 7). That means "cruel and oppressive in their disposition, and prompt and speedy in their assaults and conquests." (Adam Clarke)
- They were impetuous (impulsive and hotheaded), quick to destroy, without conscience (1:6).
- They had conquered the known earth, seizing palaces, and homes, everything they desired (1:6). They were unstoppable and most feared above all people (1:7).
- They did not respect the laws of any that they conquered. They showed no respect for the beliefs or practices of anyone but themselves (1:7).
- Their armies invaded with speed, strength, and surprise. They were masters of war with the greatest horses and weapons (1:8).
- Their army moved as one disciplined unit with one purpose, violence, and destruction (1:9). They took captives as easily as one scoops up a handful of sand in the desert (1:9).
- They mock and laugh at the nations who fall at their feet.

They reduce the greatest of palaces and armies to a pile of trash (1:10).

- They patiently build siege ramps to storm fortresses, nothing deters or stops them (1:10).

These are the people God was sending against His beloved children. Judah had to be disciplined. As the people of God, they had been commissioned to be the family line that would bring the Messiah into the world. Judah, in that sense, was the channel of the Gospel for a lost world, but they had lost their way. Strong discipline was needed for the people of God to get back on track.

One more thing in these verses that needs to be noted. God will also judge the Chaldeans. Their wickedness had not gone unnoticed. They will be held guilty and accountable for their many sins, and none of their false gods will save them.

> "They mock at kings
> And rulers are a laughing matter to them.
> They laugh at every fortress
> And heap up rubble to capture it.
> "Then they will sweep through like the wind and pass on.
> But they will be held guilty,
> They whose strength is their god." (1:10)

Habakkuk cannot understand how God could use the Babylonians to discipline His people, Judah (1:13-17).

[12] Are You not from everlasting,
O LORD, my God, my Holy One?
We will not die.
You, O LORD, have appointed them to judge;
And You, O Rock, have established them to correct.

¹³ *Your* eyes are too pure to approve evil,
And You cannot look on wickedness *with favor*.
Why do You look with favor
On those who deal treacherously?
Why are You silent when the wicked swallow up
Those more righteous than they?
¹⁴ *Why* have You made men like the fish of the sea,
Like creeping things without a ruler over them?
¹⁵ *The Chaldeans* bring all of them up with a hook,
Drag them away with their net,
And gather them together in their fishing net.
Therefore they rejoice and are glad.
¹⁶ Therefore they offer a sacrifice to their net
And burn incense to their fishing net;
Because through these things their catch is large,
And their food is plentiful.
¹⁷ Will they therefore empty their net
And continually slay nations without sparing?

Habakkuk was stunned beyond words. In his mind, it didn't seem possible that God could do this. Of course, Habakkuk knew God was right in all He did but it was troubling. Judah may have sinned and done evil in the eyes of God, but Babylon was a pagan nation. So, Habakkuk proceeded to question God. How could He use a nation more wicked than Judah to discipline His people?

Habakkuk added to God's list everything he could think of about the terrible empire. Everything Habakkuk listed was true about Babylon. Have you ever questioned God? Have you wondered why God allowed something to happen? God was patient with Habakkuk's questions, and He is patient with our questions. God can do anything He wants. He is always right.

Habakkuk was wrong in several things. He said what God

planned would not happen, *"O Lord, my God, my Holy One, we will not die"* (1:12). Habakkuk thought he understood God and nobody would die. That would be an evil thing. Habakkuk then reasoned that if the wicked Chaldeans did invade and destroy the land and capture the people, then God is somehow looking at the Babylonian empire with more favor than His people.

> **"You, O Lord, have appointed them to judge;**
> **And You, O Rock, have established them to correct.**
> **Your eyes are too pure to approve evil,**
> **And You cannot look on wickedness with favor.**
> **Why do You look with favor**
> **On those who deal treacherously?**
> **Why are You silent when the wicked swallow up**
> **Those more righteous than they?"** (1:12, 13)

In Habakkuk's mind, Judah should be the one to judge Babylon, not the other way around. Babylon was the personification of evil and God is everything good. God cannot approve of evil so how can He use them against the chosen of God, Judah (1:13)? How can God show His favor on sinners? How can He remain silent when a people more wicked than Judah swallow them up? Habakkuk concluded that God saw Babylon as more righteous than Judah. In this case, was the cure worse than the disease?

The prophet then acknowledged God made all men, even the Babylonians. He then sees Judah like helpless fish in the sea. Babylon will come to cast their nets and gather up all the fish. Then after taking their catch of fish out of the net, the pagan nation offers sacrifices to the net. In their idolatry, they have no God to give credit for the victory, so they burn incense in worship to the net (1:14-17). In all this, God appears silent. Will God have no mercy on His helpless fish? It was true they had sinned but is sending the Babylonians a righteous way to judge?

Habakkuk thought he knew God but he didn't. Job, in his book, had the same experience. He also thought he knew God, but later learned how little he knew. After God showed Job what he didn't know, this was Job's response:

> "Then Job answered the LORD and said,
> 'I know that You can do all things,
> And that no purpose of Yours can be thwarted.
> Who is this that hides counsel without knowledge?'
> Therefore I have declared that which I did not understand,
> Things too wonderful for me, which I did not know."
> Hear, now, and I will speak;
> I will ask You, and You instruct me.'
> I have heard of You by the hearing of the ear;
> But now my eye sees You;
> Therefore I retract,
> And I repent in dust and ashes.'" (Job 42:1-8)

Habakkuk was about to learn the same lesson:

> "For as the heavens are higher than the earth, So are My ways higher than your ways And My thoughts than your thoughts." (Isaiah 55:9)

To learn that lesson he needed to be silent and listen for a while. That is not a bad thing to do for any of us who are angry or frustrated at the evil around us that seems to be winning. Where is God when bad things happen to good people? It is a great time to be quiet and wait for the answer from God.

IMPORTANT INSIGHT.

Habakkuk believed that compared to his people of Judah, the Babylonians were wicked. He saw his countrymen as more righteous than the wicked sinners God was going to use as His instrument of discipline for Judah. He viewed his people as God's people and therefore good people, even though they had themselves sinned. But all sin is an abomination to God. There is no

17

"good" sin. The Bible is clear, there is none righteous, no not one.

We are born in sin and live in sin. We are all as an unclean thing (see Romans 3:10-18). In other words, a bad thing was not going to happen to good people. There are no good people, just forgiven and redeemed people. Only God is good; that is what Jesus said.
Here is the insight. Only one time in the history of the universe has a bad thing happened to a good person. That was when all the filth and vile sins of all of us were put on the sinless Lamb of God on the cross!

Habakkuk Two

Habakkuk becomes silent and waits for God's answer (2:1).

I will stand on my guard post
And station myself on the rampart;
And I will keep watch to see what He will speak to me,
And how I may reply when I am reproved.

We have seen that Habakkuk was confused and frustrated. It seemed like God was indifferent. Habakkuk was not accusing God, he just wanted to understand what was happening. The only One who could answer that was God. Habakkuk wisely closed his mouth and went up to a guard post on the Jerusalem city wall by himself and waited on God. Habakkuk expected to be reproved by God but he needed to know.

God answers Habakkuk in a vision that contained a message for Judah (2:2, 3).

² Then the LORD answered me and said,
"Record the vision
And inscribe *it* on tablets,
That the one who reads it may run.
³ "For the vision is yet for the appointed time;
It hastens toward the goal and it will not fail.
Though it tarries, wait for it;
For it will certainly come, it will not delay.

God showed up in a vision. He confirmed everything He had told Habakkuk was going to happen. The appointed time was coming for the Babylonian invasion (2:3). Habakkuk was to write down the prophecy on tablets, a common way important documents were kept in that time (2:2). Habakkuk knew Judah deserved the punishment God was sending. They had abandoned God and followed false gods. They abused the poor and the widow. The courts were corrupted and the poor of the nation were powerless and neglected. They did not allow the land to rest every seven years according to the Law of Moses (Leviticus 25:1-4). Because they had ignored that instruction from God for 70 times (over 490 years), God had the nation taken captive for 70 years to allow the land to rest and teach the people that His Word must be followed.

The vision was clear, the judgment was appointed and it would not fail or be delayed (2:3). He said to leave a permanent warning in stone so that those who choose to turn back to God could do so. He was to write the prophecy clearly so anyone could read it. The word "*run*" is a little confusing (2:2). It does not seem to mean running like in a race or fleeing from something. The Jewish Targum says, *"write the prophecy, and explain it in the book of the law, that he may hasten to obtain wisdom, whoever he is that reads it.*" The Jewish Commentary, the Targum, sees the Hebrew word as meaning a person who reads the prophecy could easily run through the document without stopping, it was a clear and easy thing to read. The word "inscribe" just before the phrase about running is often translated as "make it plain." Hebrew parallelism groups several sentences together that say the same thing to make them clear and emphasize the importance of the statement. These two parallel sentences build on each other. Habakkuk was to make the message in stone in a plain and easy to read fashion so the everyday citizen of Judah could hear the message. Even the least learned could easily run through the text. The message was not just for the elite or the priests, but everyman was to get the warning. God then completes the vision with a message about Babylon.

God will also judge the proud Babylonians (2:4-8).

⁴ "Behold, as for the proud one,
His soul is not right within him;
But the righteous will live by his faith.
⁵ "Furthermore, wine betrays the haughty man,
So that he does not stay at home.
He enlarges his appetite like Sheol,
And he is like death, never satisfied.
He also gathers to himself all nations
And collects to himself all peoples.
⁶ "Will not all of these take up a taunt-song against him,
Even mockery and insinuations against him
And say, 'Woe to him who increases what is not his—
For how long—
And makes himself rich with loans?'
⁷ "Will not your creditors rise up suddenly,

And those who collect from you awaken?
Indeed, you will become plunder for them.
[8] "Because you have looted many nations,
All the remainder of the peoples will loot you—
Because of human bloodshed and violence done to the land,
To the town and all its inhabitants.

The first part of the vision was for Judah but it did not answer the heartache of Habakkuk. How could God use the wicked Babylonians to judge His people in Judah? It seemed like the only ones being judged were the people of God and the arrogant Chaldean people were getting a free pass. The second part of the vision tells the whole story. God will judge all sin. He would take care of Babylon also.

God revealed to Habakkuk that Babylon would face the wrath of God. Even though judgment began with Judah, it did not end there. In verses 4-8, God began to address the sins of Babylon. He starts with the root of sin, pride.

> **"Behold, as for the proud one,**
> **His soul is not right within him."** (2:4)

Pride is the beginning of sin. The first sin was Lucifer's who believed he could be like God. He said, *'I will ascend above the heights of the clouds; I will make myself like the Most High."* (Isaiah 14:14). Then, the first couple brought sin into the human race when they disobeyed God following Satan's original lie, "The serpent said to the woman, *'You surely will not die! For God knows that in the day you eat from it your eyes will be opened, and you will be like God, knowing good and evil'"* (Genesis 3:4). The same root sin of pride caused Lucifer's fall, Adam and Eve's disobedience in the garden, and the actions of Babylon. In this passage, God addressed Babylon as "the proud one."

"**Pride is a strange creature; it never objects to its lodgings. It will live comfortably enough in a palace, and it will live equally at its ease in a slum. Is there any man in whose heart pride does not lurk?**" (Spurgeon)

Habakkuk was concerned that Babylon would get away with their sin. That was not going to happen. God knew that their soul was not right within them (2:4). Pride says, "I am the most important." Pride has been described as the "only disease that makes everyone sick except the person who has it!" We do know that pride never ends well. *"God resists the proud but gives grace to the humble"* (Proverbs 3:34; James 4:6). So, when God began His judgment against Babylon with the words, "*Behold, as for the proud one,*" we know it will not end well.

The opposite of pride is humility, humble dependence upon God. In other words, faith is what God desires, not arrogant independence. Our lives are to be marked by trusting God, having faith in Him. The last part of this poetic parallelism gives the opposite statement, opposite from the man of pride, "*But the righteous will live by his faith.*" This simple little verse is an enormous statement. Before we look at just how important it is, remember our three types of parallelism? There is **synonymous**, where statements say the same thing. There is **antithetic** where statements say the opposite and **synthetic** where multiple lines together complete the poetic statement. This one verse has a form of all three. Look at the verse again:

> "**Behold, as for the proud one,
> His soul is not right within him;
> But the righteous will live by his faith.**" (2:4)

The first two sentences say the same thing, the second defines the first. The third line is the opposite of the proud man, the man of faith. These three verses combine to make one statement about not just Babylon, but all men. Now, let us look at that last part.

22

"THE JUST SHALL LIVE BY HIS FAITH" (2:4).

Habakkuk is more known by this one line than anything else he said. It is quoted in three New Testament books: Romans, Hebrews, and Galatians. It is interesting to note that there are three elements in the sentence. There is the "*just,*" the righteous man. Then there is "*shall live*" the Christian life. Finally, there is "*faith*", without which a man cannot be saved. Each of the quotations in the New Testament focus on a different element when they quote Habakkuk 2:4.

1. Romans 1:17 focuses on *the* justified man – "The *just* shall live by faith."
2. Galatians 3:11 focuses on the Christian life – "The just shall *live* by faith."
3. Hebrews 10:38 focuses on our faith – "The just shall live by *faith.*"

"THE JUST SHALL LIVE BY FAITH"

A CATHOLIC MONK THAT HELPED CHANGE THE WORLD.

It was the words, "The just shall live by his faith" that began the Protestant Reformation in the early sixteenth century in Europe. Many refer to this era as the "dark ages of the church." Leaders of the church had become rich and powerful. Spiritual darkness had infected the soul of the church and specifically one priest named Martin Luther.

Martin Luther struggled for years to lead a life that would please God Who would grant him eternal life. The more he struggled, the more lost he felt. He religiously performed all the pilgrimages, kept the Sacraments, climbed and kissed sacred stairs, prayed the Rosary faithfully, and many other practices. But nothing brought peace to his troubled soul. He began to hate the description of God as being *"Righteous."* To Martin Luther, it meant that God will punish all the unrighteous and that meant everyone, including himself. There was no way out of his spiritual struggle. All men are trapped in their sinful natures and no amount of good works can ever be adequate to measure up to God's perfection, God's righteousness.

Martin Luther happened to be teaching the book of Galatians when he came across Paul's quote from Habakkuk used in Galatians 3:11, *"The righteous (just) shall live by faith."* He was stunned and realized he had no answer to that. He had worked and worked to become righteous by his works, his good deeds, and following all the rules of the church. We will let Martin Luther describe what happened to him next:

> **"Though I lived as a monk without reproach, I felt that I was a sinner before God...I did not love, yes, I hated the righteous God who punishes sinners...Thus I raged with a fierce and troubled conscience. Nevertheless, I beat importunately upon Paul at that place...desiring to know what St. Paul wanted. At last, by the mercy of God, meditating day and night, I gave heed to the context of the words, namely, in it, the righteousness of God is revealed, as it is written, 'He who through faith is righteous shall live.' There I began to understand that the righteousness of God is that by which the righteous lives by a gift of God, namely by faith...it is the righteousness of God revealed by the gospel, that is, the passive righteousness with which merciful God justifies us by faith...Here I felt that I was altogether born again and had entered paradise itself through open gates...And I extolled my sweetest word with**

a love as great as the hatred with which I had before hated the word 'righteousness of God.' Thus, that place in Paul was for me truly the gate to paradise."
(Luther's works, vol. 34: Career of the Reformer IV)

That one verse was the seed, it was faith alone that makes a man righteous. In that one sentence from Habakkuk, a spiritual earthquake happened in the church of Rome and it ended up shaking the world. *"The just shall live by faith."*

**"Behold, as for the proud one,
His soul is not right within him;
But the righteous will live by his faith.** (2:4)

The pride of the Babylonians would be brought low, just as all pride will one day be crushed. Every man will ultimately bow before the Lord.

"Being found in appearance as a man, He humbled Himself by becoming obedient to the point of death, even death on a cross. For this reason also, God highly exalted Him, and bestowed on Him the name which is above every name, so that at the name of Jesus every knee will bow, of those who are in heaven and on earth and under the earth, and that every tongue will confess that Jesus Christ is Lord, to the glory of God the Father."
(Philippians 2:8-11)

BABYLON'S LUST FOR POWER CANNOT BE SATISFIED (2:5-8).

The lust for power is never quenched. A very rich man was once asked, "How much is enough?" He responded, "Just a little bit more." God compares Babylon's lust for power to an alcoholic who cannot get enough drink.

> **"Furthermore, wine betrays the haughty man,**
> **So that he does not stay at home.**
> **He enlarges his appetite like Sheol,**
> **And he is like death, never satisfied.**
> **He also gathers to himself all nations**
> **And collects to himself all peoples."** (2:5)

The drunk abandons his family. His addiction drives him from his home to satisfy his cravings. His appetite for a drink is never satisfied no matter where he goes. Just as Sheol, the grave, is never satisfied, it continually grows. The grave never says, "that is enough, no more deaths now, I am full." The Alcoholic never says, "That last drink was the one I needed and now I will stop drinking." Babylon never says, "we have enough land, slaves, wealth, and power." No, Babylon *also gathers to himself all nations and collects to himself all peoples* (2:5). That lust will never be satisfied.

It was helpful for Habakkuk to hear from God. The evil things Babylon had done will come back to destroy them.

> **"He who digs a pit will fall into it,**
> **And he who rolls a stone, it will come back on him."**
> (Proverbs 26:27)

The next verses (2:6-8) describe the time when Babylon will reap the harvest they have sown. Their end was coming. Babylon plundered, looted, and made many nations poor. They will be treated the same way. They will meet their doom. The people who have been harmed and robbed will one day see the fall of Babylon and sing a song mocking the fallen, wicked empire. Verses six through eight is the song they will sing on that day:

> **"Will not all of these take up a taunt-song against him,**
> **Even mockery and insinuations against him**
> **And say, 'Woe to him who increases what is not his—**
> **For how long—**

And makes himself rich with loans?'
"Will not your creditors rise up suddenly,
And those who collect from you awaken?
Indeed, you will become plunder for them.
"Because you have looted many nations,
All the remainder of the peoples will loot you—
Because of human bloodshed and violence done
to the land,
To the town and all its inhabitants. (2:6-8)

Verse eight reveals that the looting of the land by Babylon was very violent. Here is how one commentary describes what was happening:

> "The Chaldeans may have made Lebanon their
> hunting-ground, and possibly they carried the chase to
> excess, though "spoil" or destruction does not mean
> extermination but violent treatment. The earth, the
> woods, and the beasts no less than man have rights; there
> is nothing that exists which is not moral; wanton excess
> on anything recoils on the head of the perpetrator. The
> ravage and terror carried into the world of creatures shall
> come back in terror and destruction on the Chaldean."
> (Cambridge Bible for Schools and Colleges)

The charges have been made first against Judah, then Babylon. Next, Habakkuk will deliver a series of four woe oracles, pronouncements of doom that are coming to Babylon.

Four woe oracles are preached against the Babylonians (2:9-14).

INTRODUCTION TO THE FOUR WOES.

These woes are against any society that violates the principles of the Word of God. Judah was going to be destroyed by the

Babylonians because they had abandoned God. Even though these woes are addressed to Babylon they deal with general sins of greed, violence, pride, false security, and idolatry. In Habakkuk's day, no nation was innocent of these sins. We could say the same today.

> **"How remarkably modern these 'woes' seem even though they were written to describe the ancient Babylonian culture at the time of Habakkuk. The Babylonians looked to their own manmade gods and military power to give them security, which they sought to attain by a total disregard for the rights and dignity of others."**
> (David Jeremiah)

Woe oracle one (2:6, 9-11).
THE FATE OF THE GREEDY.

9 "Woe to him who gets evil gain for his house
To put his nest on high,
To be delivered from the hand of calamity!
10 "You have devised a shameful thing for your house
By cutting off many peoples;
So you are sinning against yourself.
11 "Surely the stone will cry out from the wall,
And the rafter will answer it from the framework.

Habakkuk manages to describe the horror of sin and God's judgment in beautiful poetry. In this first of his woe oracles, the problem of greed and ill-gotten gain is addressed. The previous verses introduced this first of the woes, *'Woe to him who increases what is not his" (2:6).* The people had engaged in devious practices to secure personal safety. They ended up putting their families at risk instead of protecting them. The end (personal protection) does not justify the means (greedy business practices). By attempting to protect his interests, *"To put his nest on high, to be delivered from the hand of calamity!"*

28

(2:9), he humiliated himself and his people. The evidence of his greedy life will *"cry out." It* will be seen by everyone. The very stones and structure of the fancy homes built by the greedy stand as a public testimony of the selfish and corrupt way they got it.

> **"So, you are sinning against yourself.**
> **"Surely the stone will cry out from the wall,**
> **And the rafter will answer it from the framework."** (2:11)

The absolute selfishness of a greedy life is only about helping oneself with no thought of helping others. The result is the *"cutting off of many peoples"* (2:10). We have already seen how God rebukes the proud. Pride leads to greed, it is all about a person taking care of himself above everything else.

> **"There is a lawful gain, which, by the blessing of God, may be a comfort to a house; but what is got by fraud and injustice, will bring poverty and ruin upon a family. Yet that is not the worst; You have sinned against your soul, have endangered it. Those who wrong their neighbors, do much greater wrong to their souls."**
> (Matthew Henry)

In the end, it all comes to nothing. Jesus later warned about this very thing:

> **"And He told them a parable, saying, The land of a rich man was very productive. And he began reasoning to himself, saying, 'What shall I do, since I have no place to store my crops?' Then he said, 'This is what I will do: I will tear down my barns and build larger ones, and there I will store all my grain and my goods. And I will say to my soul, "Soul, you have many goods laid up for many years to come; take your ease, eat, drink and be merry."' But God said to him, 'You fool! This very night your soul is required of you; and now who will own what you have prepared?' So is the man who stores up treasure for himself, and is not rich toward God."** (Luke 12:16-21)

Woe to all who seek ill-gotten gain and practice inhumanity in that pursuit.

Woe oracle two (2:12-14).

BUILDING WITH VIOLENCE.

12 "Woe to him who builds a city with bloodshed
And founds a town with violence!
13 "Is it not indeed from the LORD of hosts
That peoples toil for fire,
And nations grow weary for nothing?
14 "For the earth will be filled
With the knowledge of the glory of the LORD,
As the waters cover the sea.

The first woe described a man who built his house with stones of greed. This woe is about the one who built a monument to himself through violence and bloodshed. This a trusted prince or leader who builds a city for his glory, not for the glory of God. In the end, the works of his hand will be destroyed with fire (2:12, 13). The Psalmist speaks of the same thing:

> "Unless the Lord builds the house,
> They labor in vain who build it;
> Unless the Lord guards the city,
> The watchman keeps awake in vain." (Psalm 127:1)

Only that which is built for God will survive the fire, will endure. The nations of the world will one day be as nothing, their efforts to build empires will be brought to nothing (2:13).

> "Behold, the nations are like a drop from a bucket,
> And are regarded as a speck of dust on the scales;
> Behold, He lifts up the islands like fine dust.

> Even Lebanon is not enough to burn,
> Nor its beasts enough for a burnt offering.
> All the nations are as nothing before Him,
> They are regarded by Him as less than nothing and
> meaningless." (Isaiah 40:15-17)

Just as the great oceans are filled with water, so in the end, the glory of God will fill all things and the feeble works of man will be forgotten (2:13, 14). Jesus said something about this as well:

> "Therefore everyone who hears these words of Mine and acts on them, may be compared to a wise man who built his house on the rock. And the rain fell, and the floods came, and the winds blew and slammed against that house; and yet it did not fall, for it had been founded on the rock. Everyone who hears these words of Mine and does not act on them, will be like a foolish man who built his house on the sand. The rain fell, and the floods came, and the winds blew and slammed against that house; and it fell—and great was its fall." (Matthew 7:24-27)

Woe to all who use violence against others to fulfill their lusts.

Woe oracle three (2:15-17).

DRUNKEN DECEPTION.

15 "Woe to you who make your neighbors drink,
Who mix in your venom even to make *them* drunk
So as to look on their nakedness!
16 "You will be filled with disgrace rather than honor.
Now you yourself drink and expose your *own* nakedness.
The cup in the LORD's right hand will come around
to you,
And utter disgrace *will come* upon your glory.

¹⁷ "For the violence done to Lebanon will overwhelm you,
And the devastation of *its* beasts by which you terrified
them,
Because of human bloodshed and violence done to the land,
To the town and all its inhabitants.

"Be of sober spirit, be on the alert. Your adversary, the
devil, prowls around like a roaring lion, seeking someone
to devour." (1 Peter 5:8)

Dangerous times require a sober mind and alertness to the
threats around us. This third woe is a strong warning about
drunkenness and the disgrace that was coming while the people
were partying instead of preparing. Verse 15 hints at a
connection between drunkenness and immorality, which can
more easily take place when resistance is weakened.

Babylon was a powerful empire but the book of Daniel reveals
that drunken festivals were a way of life for them. Daniel gives
us a window into the Babylonian practices:

"Belshazzar the king held a great feast for a thousand of
his nobles, and he was drinking wine in the presence of
the thousand. When Belshazzar tasted the wine, he gave
orders to bring the gold and silver vessels which
Nebuchadnezzar his father had taken out of the temple
which was in Jerusalem, so that the king and his nobles,
his wives and his concubines might drink from them.
Then they brought the gold vessels that had been taken
out of the temple, the house of God which was in
Jerusalem; and the king and his nobles, his wives and his
concubines drank from them. They drank the wine and
praised the gods of gold and silver, of bronze, iron, wood
and stone." (Daniel 5:1-4)

"Drink was a factor in the downfall of the Babylonian
empire. Belshazzar, in his debauched drunken orgy,
cursed God, and he mocked God in blasphemy and
sacrilege . . . 'In that night was Belshazzar the king of the

Chaldeans slain. And Darius the Mede took the kingdom."
(Preach the Word commentary)

We are exhorted in God's Word to be sober and vigilant. There is a final description of the plunder of Babylon against the northern region (See 2:8) which had terrified the people of Lebanon. The northern region of Lebanon was a prime place for the looting of the cedar forests. Babylon used the wood, as did other nations, for building palaces and temples. The Temple in Jerusalem was built with cedars from Lebanon. When Babylon looted the cedars, they did it with violence to the land and the animals. The northern region of Israel was a prime hunting ground for wild animals, or beasts, which was used by both the Assyrians and Babylonians.

"For the violence done to Lebanon will overwhelm you, And the devastation of its beasts by which you terrified them, Because of human bloodshed and violence done to the land, To the town and all its inhabitants." (2:17)

The point that Habakkuk was making to Babylon was that the horrible destruction and bloodshed they used against the people in Lebanon were coming back on them.

> "Woe to those who are wise in their own eyes
> And clever in their own sight!
> Woe to those who are heroes in drinking wine
> And valiant men in mixing strong drink," (Isaiah 5:21, 22)

Woe to those who fail to remain vigilant and spend days in drunkenness.

Woe oracle four (2:18-20).

IDOL WORSHIP.

18 "What profit is the idol when its maker has carved it,
Or an image, a teacher of falsehood?
For *its* maker trusts in his *own* handiwork
When he fashions speechless idols.
19 "Woe to him who says to a *piece of* wood, 'Awake!'
To a mute stone, 'Arise!'
And that is *your* teacher?
Behold, it is overlaid with gold and silver,
And there is no breath at all inside it.
20 "But the LORD is in His holy temple.
Let all the earth be silent before Him."

This final woe is a warning to Babylon about the foolishness of idolatry. Statues of wood and stone are just that, there is no life or hope in them. Today, many don't worship stone idols but we have developed new idols that are just as hollow. We can serve work, money, prestige, anything that consumes our passion that is not God can quickly become idolatry.

Even though Habakkuk was recording God's judgment against Babylon, the people of Judah would have seen themselves as well.

> **"Through it all, the point is proven. Habakkuk couldn't understand why God would judge a sinful nation (Judah) by an even more sinful nation (Babylon). Yet God reminds Habakkuk of His own wisdom and strength, and of His ultimate triumph over the wicked. God knew that Babylon was filled with the proud, the greedy, the violent, the drunk, and the idolater – and the LORD knew how to deal with them all."** (Enduring Word Commentary)

Those pieces of wood and rock, without breath or life (2:19), would fail and pass away. The living God would never pass away. He is God.

> **"But the Lord is in His holy temple.**
> **Let all the earth be silent before Him."** (2:20)

Woe to those who substitute wood and stone for the True and Everlasting God.

Habakkuk Three

Introduction to chapter three.

Have you ever seen a stage play where the scene was dark? When that scene was over, the stage lights came on full of brilliant colors. The darkness had ended, the scene shifted to another place. This is Habakkuk in chapter three. The dinginess of sin flooded the scene in chapter two. God would judge His people for their unfaithfulness and then He would bring His wrath against the wicked, idolatrous Babylonian empire. Woe to those who bring about the holy anger of the God of heaven and earth. Habakkuk listened in stunned silence from his watchtower on the wall. The Lord was in His holy temple and all the earth needed to be silent before Him (2:20).

Now it was Habakkuk's turn to make a sound. He prayed and praised God even when he didn't understand. It is a good time to take off your sandals. You have arrived at the burning bush. You have come to Habakkuk chapter three.

The prophet cries out to God for mercy (3:1, 2).

¹ A prayer of Habakkuk the prophet, according to Shigionoth.
² Lᴏʀᴅ, I have heard the report about You *and* I fear.
O Lᴏʀᴅ, revive Your work in the midst of the years,
In the midst of the years make it known;
In wrath remember mercy.

Shigionoth. The word is only used twice in the Bible. Habakkuk 3:1 and when David used it in Psalm seven. The meaning is not understood by Hebrew scholars.
Here is Psalm 7:1:

> "A Shiggaion of David, which he sang to the LORD
> concerning Cush, a Benjamite.
> O LORD my God, in You I have taken refuge;
> Save me from all those who pursue me, and deliver me."
> (Psalm 7:1)

For David, it was a song of praise and desperation. Maybe that is the definition. Habakkuk said he prayed according to the way of Shigionoth (the word "Shiggaion" used by David is a form of same word used by Habakkuk). His prayer was one of worship and a holy fear of God. It was also an appeal for mercy (3:2). We can guess that it was a style of singing or poetry that encompassed the deepest of emotions and appeal to God. The Hebrew word that is the root of shigionaoth is "*shagah*" which means to stray or wander off the path. That may also be a hint of the style or nature of the song. The use of "Selah" three times is also a hint of the musical nature of the chapter. Selah means pause or rest. It is like a musical rest to stop and take in what has transpired up to that point. Selah means "stop and think about it." The end of chapter three gives one more hint that this entire chapter was meant to be sung:

> **"For the choir director, on my stringed instruments."**
> (3:19)

Habakkuk begins his song of great emotion to God, telling Him how he has heard of the things God has done. It brought fear to his heart. Since "*the fear of the Lord is the beginning of wisdom*" (Proverbs 1:7), that was a good place to start.

> **"Lord, I have heard the report about You and I fear.**
> **O Lord, revive Your work in the midst of the years,**
> **In the midst of the years make it known;**
> **In wrath remember mercy."** (3:2)

Habakkuk can only appeal to the mercy of God. Like Job, Habakkuk had come to the place where he has bowed in reverence to God. He trusts what he cannot fully understand but he knows God alone is God. He prays for the revival of the work of God again. Sin has separated God from His called-out people and Habakkuk wants God to bless His people again as He did at first. He appeals to God to remember mercy in the midst of His wrath.

Have we come to the point in our lives that we are desperate for God?

The deliverance from Egypt by Moses is retold (3:3, 4).

3 God comes from Teman,
And the Holy One from Mount Paran. Selah.
His splendor covers the heavens,
And the earth is full of His praise.
4 *His* radiance is like the sunlight;
He has rays *flashing* from His hand,
And there is the hiding of His power.

This description of the Lord's appearance sounds familiar. The cry of the Hebrew children was heard by God and he sent Moses to lead them from slavery to freedom. Along the journey to the Promised Land, God led them to Mount Sinai in the southern desert of Edom, below the land of Canaan. From Mount Sinai, God appeared in great power and gave the Law to the people. Just before Moses died, he addressed the people and blessed them. Listen to his words:

> **"Now this is the blessing with which Moses the man of God blessed the sons of Israel before his death. He said,**
> **'The Lord came from Sinai,**
> **And dawned on them from Seir;**
> **He shone forth from Mount Paran,**
> **And He came from the midst of ten thousand holy ones;**
> **At His right hand there was flashing lightning for them.'"**
> (Deuteronomy 33:1, 2)

Habakkuk references the Deuteronomy blessing. Both Habakkuk and Moses used parallelism. Moses equated Mount Paran to Mount Sinai. Habakkuk equated Teman to Mount Paran. Moses and Habakkuk were both talking about the same place. All of these places are in the land of Edom, south of Israel.

Notice how one historian links all the places together:

> **"As close relatives of other *Levantine Semites*, they may have worshiped such gods as *El, Baal, Qaus* and Asherah. The oldest biblical traditions place *Yahweh* as the deity of southern Edom, and may have originated in "Edom/Seir/Teman/Sinai" before being adopted in Israel and Judah"** (*M. Leuenberger (2017). "YHWH's Provenance from the South". In J. van Oorschot; M. Witte (eds.).* The Origins of Yahwism*)

Edom was south of Judah and extended to Egypt. It was the location of Mount Sinai, also called Mount Paran. God spoke to His people there, gave them the Law, the tabernacle, the priesthood, the feasts, and established them as His nation. He then led them to the land that would be theirs.

God told Habakkuk what would happen to Babylon at the end of chapter two. The next thing God told His prophet was what we just read in chapter three about the Lord delivering His people from Egyptian bondage and being with them in power on Mount Sinai. How are these two things connected?

> **"Habakkuk's use of similar phrases connects his song of praise with Moses' blessing. Habakkuk praises God's sovereign power and ability to provide a 'second exodus' for His people—not from Egypt but from Babylon."** (God Questions)

In chapter three, God reminded Habakkuk that just as He had delivered His children from Egypt and led them to their Promised Land, He will one day bring His children home again after a season of captivity. The ultimate fulfillment of this will be in the Millennial reign of Christ when all the remnant of Israel will be restored to their land and Christ will be their rightful King. Isaiah, Zechariah, and other prophets spoke of that great coming day.

The terror of the Lord against Israel's enemies (3:5-15).

5 Before Him goes pestilence,
And plague comes after Him.
6 He stood and surveyed the earth;
He looked and startled the nations.
Yes, the perpetual mountains were shattered,
The ancient hills collapsed.
His ways are everlasting.
7 I saw the tents of Cushan under distress,
The tent curtains of the land of Midian were trembling.

8 Did the LORD rage against the rivers,
Or *was* Your anger against the rivers,
Or *was* Your wrath against the sea,
That You rode on Your horses,
On Your chariots of salvation?
9 Your bow was made bare,
The rods of chastisement were sworn. Selah.
You cleaved the earth with rivers.
10 The mountains saw You *and* quaked;
The downpour of waters swept by.
The deep uttered forth its voice,
It lifted high its hands.
11 Sun *and* moon stood in their places;
They went away at the light of Your arrows,
At the radiance of Your gleaming spear.
12 In indignation You marched through the earth;
In anger You trampled the nations.
13 You went forth for the salvation of Your people,
For the salvation of Your anointed.
You struck the head of the house of the evil
To lay him open from thigh to neck. Selah.

¹⁴ You pierced with his own spears
The head of his throngs.
They stormed in to scatter us;
Their exultation *was* like those
Who devour the oppressed in secret.
¹⁵ You trampled on the sea with Your horses,
On the surge of many waters.

Habakkuk recounts Israel's history to the people of Judah. He shows that when God went to war against the enemies of His people, there were supernatural results. Plagues and pestilence hammered Egypt into submission (3:5). No army can withstand the day of His wrath. Nations trembled at His power and presence like at Jericho. Rahab told the spies that the people trembled at the thought of the God of the Hebrews coming to fight for His people:

> "For we have heard how the Lord dried up the water of the Red Sea before you when you came out of Egypt, and what you did to the two kings of the Amorites who were beyond the Jordan, to Sihon and Og, whom you utterly destroyed. When we heard it, our hearts melted and no courage remained in any man any longer because of you; for the Lord your God, He is God in heaven above and on earth beneath." (Joshua 2:10, 11)

Habakkuk recounts to his people the greatness of God. Even the mountains cannot stand in His presence (3:6) like at Sinai when the ground and mountains quaked. He is God from everlasting to everlasting (3:6). He was showing his people that God never changes and He can deliver His people again despite the difficult days that were coming.

> "The world is under His government, and all things in it subject to His providence; He can rule and overrule all things for His glory, and the good of His interest. He will do it; everything is subject to His control, and under His direction; not a step can be taken without His will.

41

This the prophet observes along with the above things, to encourage the faith and expectation of the saints, that the work of the Lord will be revived, and his kingdom and interest promoted and established in the world; though there may, and will, be many difficulties and distresses previous to it." (Bible Study Tools Commentary)

Many lands were conquered by the Israelites when God was with them. Cush and Midian are mentioned as examples (3:7). Verses 8-15 are a poetic series of vivid images of the power and conquests of God. He turned the river into blood in Pharaoh's time and the horse and the rider He cast into the sea destroying Pharaoh's army at the Red Sea (3:8). God was not a God sitting in Heaven but a God active with His people in the battle, He used His weapons, unsheathed His bow (3:9). He did miracles like holding back the Jordan, collapsing Jericho's walls, terrorizing the nations, and even making the sun and moon stand still in Joshua's time (3:10, 11).

> **"Then Joshua spoke to the LORD in the day when the LORD delivered up the Amorites before the sons of Israel, and he said in the sight of Israel,**
>
> > **'O sun, stand still at Gibeon,**
> > **And O moon in the valley of Aijalon.'**
>
> **So the sun stood still, and the moon stopped,**
> **Until the nation avenged themselves of their enemies.'**
> **Is it not written in the book of Jashar? And the sun stopped in the middle of the sky and did not hasten to go down for about a whole day.**
> **There was no day like that before it or after it, when the Lord listened to the voice of a man; for the Lord fought for Israel."** (Joshua 10:12-14)

God would lead the people throughout the land of Canaan, step by step, region by region, overcoming the nations, plundering, and cutting out the evil in the land.

"In indignation You marched through the earth;
In anger You trampled the nations.
You went forth for the salvation of Your people,
For the salvation of Your anointed.
You struck the head of the house of the evil
To lay him open from thigh to neck." Selah. (3:12, 13)

This entire story as we have seen is like a hymn of praise, music written to be sung for the people at the Temple. They sang the praises of how God brought salvation to the land. Then, three times during the hymn the word "Selah" is placed. A musical rest, a moment intentionally placed to tell the people, stop and think about what you are singing. Think about what all God has done for you. He will do it again.

The nations God helped Israel defeat were powerful and evil. The wars were bloody and at times went back and forth. In the end, God drove His people to victory (3:13-15). The references to the deliverance from Egypt, the pagan lands, and the claiming of the Promised Land by Joshua were meant to show the people of Judah that God will do it again after the Babylonian scourge. He is still God and even though disobedient, the people are still His covenant people.

Habakkuk accepts the will of God in difficult times (4:16).

16 I heard and my inward parts trembled,
At the sound my lips quivered.
Decay enters my bones,
And in my place I tremble.
Because I must wait quietly for the day of distress,
For the people to arise *who* will invade us.

When Habakkuk went up on his wall, sat in the watchtower, and waited on God in silence, it was then that he was ready to really listen to God. When God answered his heart's cry, it was not what he wanted to hear but it was the truth. God was sending the vicious Babylonian army to destroy the land of Judah, level the Temple of Solomon into the dust, and take the leaders and highest in the land into captivity to Mesopotamia. Later, in God's timing, He would bring judgment against Babylon for its many sins. God judges all sin; He is not a respecter of persons. *"The wages of sin is death"* (Romans 6:23) applies to all mankind.

When Habakkuk understood the holiness and justice of God, he trembled, his lips quivered (3:16). He understood what the invasion was about and he felt weak and helpless like a man whose bones were decayed. He knew, like the others, he was a sinner as well. Isaiah, after being in the presence of the Lord, said these words:

> **"Woe is me, for I am ruined!**
> **Because I am a man of unclean lips,**
> **And I live among a people of unclean lips;**
> **For my eyes have seen the King, the Lord of hosts."**
> (Isaiah 6:4)

We may not like God's answers to our prayers, but they are God's answers. Habakkuk had heard from God and he trembled (3:16). He then resolved to wait patiently on God. The day of distress was going to come, the Babylonians were preparing for the invasion. It was a time to warn the people, but mostly it was a time to accept the difficult will of God and silently praise His wisdom (3:16).

The song Habakkuk sang to God is one of the most beautiful in Scripture. Try to picture him singing to God with his heart in joyful submission and praise, even in the troubling times.

Habakkuk's hymn of praise to God (3:17-19).

17 Though the fig tree should not blossom
And there be no fruit on the vines,
Though the yield of the olive should fail
And the fields produce no food,
Though the flock should be cut off from the fold
And there be no cattle in the stalls,
18 Yet I will exult in the LORD,
I will rejoice in the God of my salvation.
19 The Lord God is my strength,
And He has made my feet like hinds' *feet*,
And makes me walk on my high places.

For the choir director, on my stringed instruments.

Habakkuk accepted that rough days were coming with the Babylonians but when he focused on God and not the destruction, he was lifted above the horror and saw the hope in God's words. The desolations in the land would rob the people of their comforts and take away their vineyards and crops. Habakkuk knew he could trust God (3:17). The cattle will be no more in the land but his God owns the cattle on a thousand hills and would be his provider (3:17). Babylon is the destroyer; God is Habakkuk's salvation (3:18). God alone will give His child the feet of the deer on the cliffs. He will not fall but be safe in his Creator's hands (3:19). The ground may look perilous under his feet but Habakkuk understood that he would walk in safety on the high places (3:19). He was in God's strong hands and that was good enough for the prophet. Then, like a great musical crescendo, the song of Habakkuk ends.

He closed the hymn with a note at the end with an instruction to the Temple music director.

45

"To the chief singer on my stringed instruments - This line, which is evidently a superscription, leads me to suppose that when the prophet had completed his short ode, he folded it up, with the above direction to the master singer, or leader of the choir, to be sung in the temple service. Many of the Psalms are directed in the same way. 'To the master singer;' or, 'chief musician;' to be sung, according to their nature, on different kinds of instruments, or with particular airs or tunes."
(Adam Clarke)

FINAL THOUGHTS.

Job was quoted in the commentary in chapter one. I can imagine Habakkuk quoting him at the end of his writing. Habakkuk was on a journey of faith through his book. He questioned God and then wisely let God speak. The prophet listened and even though the words of God were difficult to grasp, Habakkuk knew they were true and he ended his book walking securely along his mountain ledge with the feet of a deer, safely and securely, praising the God of heaven and earth. Both Job and Habakkuk went through difficult situations and both came to realize that God is in control of everything. The place of peace in troubled times was, and still is, found in walking close to God. Let's listen once more to what Job said after God showed him how little he knew about the mind of the Infinite One.

"I know that You can do all things,
And that no purpose of Yours can be thwarted.
'Who is this that hides counsel without knowledge?'
Therefore I have declared that which I did not understand,
Things too wonderful for me, which I did not know."
'Hear, now, and I will speak;
I will ask You, and You instruct me.'
"I have heard of You by the hearing of the ear;
But now my eye sees You;
Therefore I retract,
And I repent in dust and ashes." (Job 42:1-8)

"I WILL REJOICE IN THE GOD OF MY SALVATION.
THE LORD GOD IS MY STRENGTH.
AND HE HAS MADE MY FEET LIKE HINDS' FEET.
AND MAKES ME WALK ON MY HIGH PLACES."

HABAKKUK 3:18, 19

ZEPHANIAH

Judgments against the nations and the coming of the day of the LORD.

"The great day of the Lord is near, Near and coming very quickly"

Zephaniah 1:14

Introduction

Who was Zephaniah?

Zephaniah prophesied around 620 B.C. This was during the reign of Josiah, the king of Judah (640 to 609 B.C.). As a young child, Zephaniah saw the evil practices of Josiah's grandfather, the horrible king, Manasseh. In Zephaniah's lifetime, he saw the nation turn from a time of random killings, child sacrifices, and idolatry. The return of righteousness and the Law came under Josiah. Helpful historical background can be found in 2 Kings 21:16 and 2 Chronicles 33:1–10.

One of the unique features of the book of Zephaniah is the theme of the day of the Lord. Zephaniah mentions it 23 times, which is more than any other book in the Bible.

> **"It refers primarily to God's impending time of judgment on the nation of Judah. Zephaniah saw in the day of the Lord the destruction of his country, his neighbors, and eventually the whole earth (Zephaniah 1:2, 4; 2:10). Zephaniah wrote that the day of the Lord was near (1:14), that it would be a time of wrath (1:15), that it would come as a judgment on sin (1:17), and that ultimately it would result in the blessing of God's presence among His people (3:17)."** (Chuck Swindoll)

The day of the Lord had a multi-fold meaning in Zephaniah. It pointed to the judgment of Judah by the Babylonians, and it also looked forward to a day in the distant future when dramatic, world-changing events would culminate with Christ's second coming.

Zephaniah simple outline.

I. Judgment of Judah and Jerusalem, chapter one.

II. Judgment of the earth and all nations, chapters 2:1—3:8.

III. Judgments removed; God's kingdom established, chapter 3:9-20.

Zephaniah One

Introduction.

The Jewish virtual library introduces Zephaniah chapter one this stunning way:

> "Chapter one begins with a prophecy of the destruction of all life and the inhabitants of Judah and Jerusalem in particular. There is not one word of hope. No one is to be spared. The sin of the people, especially that of the leaders, is pictured in stark and graphic detail: they worship Baal and the host of heaven, they swear by their king (*malkam*; though a god rather than a human king may be referred to here), and turn away from following YHWH. This judgment speech is set within the framework of an ominous portrayal of 'The Day of YHWH' in which Zephaniah carries further the concepts of Amos (5:18–20) and Isaiah (2:6–22). This day, portrayed as the day of YHWH's sacrifice, will be a day of utter darkness and gloom, whose sound of howling and wailing stands in sharp contrast to the silence with which the people are called into YHWH's presence:
> 'Hush before the Lord YHWH.'" (1:7)
> (Jewish Virtual Library)

Zephaniah is introduced (1;1).

¹ The word of the LORD which came to Zephaniah son of Cushi, son of Gedaliah, son of Amariah, son of Hezekiah, in the days of Josiah son of Amon, king of Judah:

> "It appears to be quite obvious that Zephaniah's reason for including so many of his ancestors in this verse was for the purpose of indicating his royal descent from the good king Hezekiah of Judah. It is barely possible that there could have been another reason. His father was Cushi, which means "an Ethiopian or a Cushite." The offspring resulting from a Hebrew girl's marrying a foreigner" would not have been accepted in the Jewish community unless he could show a pure Jewish pedigree for at lease three generations (Deuteronomy 23:8)." (Coffman's Commentaries on the Bible)

> "You shall not loathe an Edomite, for he is your brother; you shall not loathe an Egyptian (Cushite), because you were a stranger in his land. The sons of the third generation who are born to them may enter the assembly of the Lord." (Deuteronomy 23:7, 8)

The next section (1:2-13) contains five different judgments against Judah. Here is the overall passage to read. Then we will examine each of the five judgments separately.

The day of judgment on Judah (1:2-13).

² "I will completely remove all *things*
From the face of the earth," declares the LORD.
³ "I will remove man and beast;
I will remove the birds of the sky
And the fish of the sea,
And the ruins along with the wicked;
And I will cut off man from the face of the earth," declares the LORD.

4 "So I will stretch out My hand against Judah
And against all the inhabitants of Jerusalem.
And I will cut off the remnant of Baal from this place, *And*
the names of the idolatrous priests along with the priests.
5 "And those who bow down on the housetops to the host of
heaven, And those who bow down *and* swear to the LORD
AND *yet* swear by Milcom,
6 And those who have turned back from following the LORD,
And those who have not sought the LORD or inquired of
Him."
7 Be silent before the Lord GOD!
For the day of the LORD is near,
For the LORD has prepared a sacrifice,
He has consecrated His guests.
8 "Then it will come about on the day of the LORD's sacrifice
That I will punish the princes, the king's sons
And all who clothe themselves with foreign garments.
9 "And I will punish on that day all who leap on the *temple*
threshold,
Who fill the house of their lord with violence and deceit.
10 "On that day," declares the LORD,
"There will be the sound of a cry from the Fish Gate,
A wail from the Second Quarter,
And a loud crash from the hills.
11 "Wail, O inhabitants of the Mortar,
For all the people of Canaan will be silenced;
All who weigh out silver will be cut off.
12 "It will come about at that time
That I will search Jerusalem with lamps,
And I will punish the men
Who are stagnant in spirit,
Who say in their hearts,
'The LORD will not do good or evil!'
13 "Moreover, their wealth will become plunder

And their houses desolate;
Yes, they will build houses but not inhabit *them*,
And plant vineyards but not drink their wine."

OVERVIEW OF THE JUDGMENTS (1:2-13).

- Zephaniah begins with God's strong pronouncement against Judah. (1:2, 3)
- Judgment is then proclaimed against the idolaters in the land. (1:4-6)
- Then the leaders and princes of the land will be judged. (1:7-9)
- The dishonest merchants are next in line for the justice of God. (1:10,11)
- All who see the evils of the land and do nothing are also guilty. (1:12, 13)

God's strong pronouncement against Judah (1:2, 3).

"'I will completely remove all things
From the face of the earth,' declares the Lord.
'I will remove man and beast;
I will remove the birds of the sky
And the fish of the sea,
And the ruins along with the wicked;
And I will cut off man from the face of the earth,' declares the Lord."

Zephaniah begins this oracle of judgment against Judah with a general pronouncement. He will later focus on different parts of the sinful nation that have incurred the wrath of God.

This word from God not only is against the sins of Judah but also points to the day of Judgment of the entire earth. God is Holy, Righteous, and Just. He will judge all sin. The people of

53

Judah, hearing this, would have understood that they were a part of that big picture, a great judgment. God will one day remove all unrepentant sinners from the earth (1:2). All the accomplishments of mankind will be destroyed. Every monument to the glory of man will be brought down (1:3). Judah will not be exempt from the wrath of God. Even the beasts, birds, and fish will be removed on that day. The book of Romans in chapter eight describes the physical world as being under the curse and groaning in pain, looking forward to the day when it will be relieved from its suffering brought on by the sin of man.

If Judah wondered why God was talking about a coming great day of judgment, they would soon understand that God was speaking to them as well. The next verses begin naming various offenses of Judah that declared them guilty.

Judgment is proclaimed against the idolaters in the land (1:4-6).

"So I will stretch out My hand against Judah
And against all the inhabitants of Jerusalem.
And I will cut off the remnant of Baal from this place,
And the names of the idolatrous priests along with the priests. And those who bow down on the housetops to the host of heaven,
And those who bow down and swear to the Lord and yet swear by Milcom,
And those who have turned back from following the Lord,
And those who have not sought the Lord or inquired of Him."

The prophets Hosea, Amos, and Isaiah spoke out against the evils of Idolatry in the Northern Kingdom of Israel. Judah would later follow in that same path and would face the same judgment. Assyria was God's instrument of discipline for the land of Israel. Babylon would take up that role against Judah. Idolatry more than any other sin violates the Great Commandment to love God above all else. Idolatry is spiritual adultery. It is telling God that the marriage between God and His people is over. They prefer to be joined to another god.

UNDERSTANDING BAAL WORSHIP.

The worst of the false gods, if one can be worse than another, was Baal. Why was Baal so important to the Canaanite region? Baal was understood to be the universal god of fertility, and in that capacity, his title was Prince, Lord of the earth. Baal was the main rival to the God of the Bible. Some worship of Baal required child sacrifice. When considering these descriptions, who else comes to mind? Who, In the Bible, is called the prince and power of the earth? Who is the destroyer of life? Who tried to be God's rival, even trying to ascend to the throne of the Almighty Himself? These are descriptions given of Satan, the destroyer.

Of all the idolatrous manifestations of the number one enemy of God, the primary one was Baal. So, when the people went after Baal, they left God to worship Satan. In the New Testament, there is a special penalty associated with taking God's glory and giving it to Satan. Mark three tells of a time when Jesus was doing miracles. The people were confused about how He could do those things. Some Jewish leaders entered the scene with their explanation:

> "The scribes who came down from Jerusalem were saying, 'He is possessed by Beelzebul,' and 'He casts out the demons by the ruler of the demons.' And He called them to Himself and began speaking to them in parables, 'How can Satan cast out Satan? If a kingdom is divided

against itself, that kingdom cannot stand. If a house is divided against itself, that house will not be able to stand. If Satan has risen up against himself and is divided, he cannot stand, but he is finished! But no one can enter the strong man's house and plunder his property unless he first binds the strong man, and then he will plunder his house.

Truly I say to you, all sins shall be forgiven the sons of men, and whatever blasphemies they utter; but whoever blasphemes against the Holy Spirit never has forgiveness, but is guilty of an eternal sin'— because they were saying, 'He has an unclean spirit.'" (Mark 3:22-30)

Who is Beelzebul? The general understanding, from many Biblical scholars and archeological sources, is that Beelzebub or Beelzebul is a name derived from a Philistine god, formerly worshipped in Ekron, and later adopted by some Abrahamic religions as a major demon. The name Beelzebub is associated with the Canaanite god Baal.

When Israel left God and served Baal, they made an eternal choice. They committed what the Bible calls the unforgivable sin. Many prophets warned God's people about this.:

> **"I am the LORD, that is My name; I will not give My glory to another, Nor My praise to graven images."** (Isaiah 42:8)

When we understand how important Baal was to the people then and what it meant, it adds a lot of meaning to the warnings in Zephaniah. Hosea had given that very warning earlier about Israel:

> **"When Ephraim spoke, there was trembling.**
> **He exalted himself in Israel,**
> **But through Baal he did wrong and died."** (13:1)

Like malignant cancer in the body, Baal worship had spread

throughout Judah. Zephaniah proclaimed that the only treatment available was radical national surgery:

> **"And I will cut off the remnant of Baal from this place,**
> **And the names of the idolatrous priests along with the**
> **priests."** (1:4)

The people worshipped many gods. They would go up on their rooftops and make offerings to the various false deities that had replaced the Creator of the heavens.

> **"And those who bow down on the housetops to the host of**
> **heaven, And those who bow down and swear to the Lord**
> **and yet swear by Milcom,**
> **And those who have turned back from following the Lord,**
> **And those who have not sought the Lord or inquired of**
> **Him."** (1:5, 6)

The Hebrew word used in verse five, "*Milcom*," can be generally translated in two ways. Its literal meaning is "their king." This would be referring to either Baal as their king or to the hosts of heaven as their king. The second possible meaning is that the word is very close to the false god Moloch, which was a well-known Canaanite god. Child sacrifice was part of the worship of Moloch. This was the pagan worship Ruth turned from in Moab to follow the Lord. Whatever evil meaning is underlying that word, the result was the same. God had to remove the cancer.

WHY IS THIS AN UNFORGIVABLE, OR UNPARDONABLE SIN?

God alone can save us. He provided eternal life by sending His beloved Son to bear our sins on the cross. When we have faith and trust Jesus as our Savior, we are "born of the spirit," or "born again." There is no other forgiveness of sin, no other pardon that can save us. If we deny God's forgiveness, we cannot find eternal life. But even worse, if we turn to Satan and worship him in place of God, then we have forever turned our back on eternal hope. The greatest insult in the universe is to reject the sacrifice of Jesus and worship the number one enemy of God. That sin can only lead to eternal separation from God. To follow Baal, after receiving the Word of God was unforgivable.

An ancient temple of Baal in Syria

The princes of the land to be judged (1:7-9).

"Be silent before the Lord God!
For the day of the Lord is near,
For the Lord has prepared a sacrifice,
He has consecrated His guests.
"Then it will come about on the day of the Lord's sacrifice
That I will punish the princes, the king's sons
And all who clothe themselves with foreign garments.

"And I will punish on that day all who leap on the temple threshold, Who fill the house of their lord with violence and deceit."

Leaders always have a greater responsibility since they can lead so many astray. The princes, the sons of the king of Judah, had used their family title in a privileged and abusive fashion. *"Righteousness exalts a nation, but sin is a disgrace to any people"* (Proverbs 14:34).

> **"When the righteous increase, the people rejoice, but when a wicked man rules, people groan."** (Proverbs 29:2)

What is particularly sad about this rebuke is that Joash, the ruling king, was listed as one of the good kings of Judah (1:1). Even though he was a good king, his children were a disgrace. They appeared to have more interest in wearing garments from other nations. It may have been a message that they were wealthy or that they associated with the pagan nations around them more than their heritage. Whether being arrogantly stylish or worldly, it reflected on the king. Joash's sons brought shame to the land. Another leader who had sons who disgraced the office of their father was Eli, the priest.

> **"Now Eli was very old; and he heard all that his sons were doing to all Israel, and how they lay with the women who served at the doorway of the tent of meeting. He said to them, 'Why do you do such things, the evil things that I hear from all these people? No, my sons; for the report is not good which I hear the Lord's people circulating. If one man sins against another, God will mediate for him; but if a man sins against the Lord, who can intercede for him?' But they would not listen to the voice of their father, for the Lord desired to put them to death."**
> (1 Samuel 2:22-25)

There was one more charge against the sons of Joash and others who followed in rebellious ways.

"And I will punish on that day all who leap on the temple threshold, Who fill the house of their lord with violence and deceit." (1:9)

The threshold of any temple had special importance to the people at that time. There is an account in 1 Samuel that gives us a hint about what it meant.

"Now the Philistines took the ark of God and brought it from Ebenezer to Ashdod. Then the Philistines took the ark of God and brought it to the house of Dagon and set it by Dagon. When the Ashdodites arose early the next morning, behold, Dagon had fallen on his face to the ground before the ark of the Lord. So they took Dagon and set him in his place again. But when they arose early the next morning, behold, Dagon had fallen on his face to the ground before the ark of the Lord. And the head of Dagon and both the palms of his hands were cut off on the threshold; only the trunk of Dagon was left to him. Therefore, neither the priests of Dagon nor all who enter Dagon's house tread on the threshold of Dagon in Ashdod to this day." (1 Samuel 5:1-5)

The priests of Dagon no longer stepped on the temple threshold after God caused the statue of Dagon to fall in the presence of the Ark of the Covenant. The threshold is the doorway, the first place you step as you enter any temple. The exact meaning of "leaping" on or over a temple threshold cannot be determined. However, since this section is directly addressing the princes of the land, then this particular act was an act of disrespect to their religious practices. Itincluded acts of violence and deceit (1:9). The sons of Joash had behaved in a fashion that disrespected their father, the king, and God.

God's word to the people was to be silent. A day of judgment was at hand. This was a time to listen to God. The people were told that God had prepared a sacrifice, a special one. God had rejected the corrupted sacrifices of His people. He proclaimed a sacrifice to cover the sins of the land. He had invited special guests to come to that sacrifice. The guests would be the Babylonians and the one to be sacrificed is Judah to atone for her multitude of sins. Read the passage again. The sacrifice is not a worship time or a time of forgiveness which are the two purposes of the Temple sacrifices. This one is a punishment:

> **"Be silent before the Lord God!**
> **For the day of the Lord is near,**
> **For the Lord has prepared a sacrifice,**
> **He has consecrated His guests.**
> **Then it will come about on the day of the Lord's sacrifice**
> **That I will punish the princes, the king's sons."** (1:7, 8)

The princes mocked the sacrificial system God established (1:8), which was a picture of the coming final sacrifice of the Lamb of God. The sons of King Joash had become a shame to the king and the nation.

> **"For if we go on sinning willfully after receiving the knowledge of the truth, there no longer remains a sacrifice for sins."** (Hebrews 10:26)

The only remaining sacrifice for sin was the nation itself. The wages of sin is death, and it was now theirs to pay since they had rejected God's way. The day of the Lord for them had arrived (1:8). The judgment does begin with the house of God and it had begun.

The dishonest merchants will face the justice of God (1:10, 11).

"¹⁰ On that day," declares the Lord,
"There will be the sound of a cry from the Fish Gate,
A wail from the Second Quarter,
And a loud crash from the hills.
"¹¹ Wail, O inhabitants of the Mortar,
For all the people of Canaan will be silenced;
All who weigh out silver will be cut off."

The day of the Lord's judgment by the Babylonian invasion and captivity will be the end of unjust business practices. Those who trust in gaining silver will be cut off (1:11). The judgment will bring a wailing of the merchants. The wail will be heard by all the nations of Canaan (1:11). From the places of commerce in the gates of the city to the hills, the cry will be heard and felt. (1:10). It would be a great lesson to all who trust in riches, especially ill-gotten wealth that had become a way of life in Judah.

The fish gate was where fish were brought in from Galilee and the Jordon. The fish market was near the gate. The sounds of crashing and wailing will be heard when the Babylonians enter through the gates and destroy the merchandise along with the city.

> **"He who trusts in his riches will fall, But the righteous will flourish like the green leaf."** (Proverbs 11:28)

The word translated "*mortar*" (1:11) is a Hebrew word that meant the "hollow place." Maktesh = "a mortar" or deep hollow, a hollow or valley evidently in the greater Jerusalem area" (Strong's concordance). God is describing those who lived in the lower part of the city, the valley of Kidron, where much of the corrupt business practices took place.

The prophet Amos also spoke out against the abuses of the poor and the unjust scales in the markets when he rebuked the Northern Kingdom of Israel. Those same corrupt practices were being used in the Southern Kingdom of Judah in Zephaniah's time. Here is the warning Amos gave to Israel:

> "Hear this, you who trample the needy, to do away with the humble of the land, saying, 'When will the new moon be over,
> So that we may sell grain,
> And the sabbath, that we may open the wheat market,
> To make the bushel smaller and the shekel bigger,
> And to cheat with dishonest scales,
> So as to buy the helpless for money
> And the needy for a pair of sandals,
> And that we may sell the refuse of the wheat?'
> "The Lord has sworn by the pride of Jacob,
> Indeed, I will never forget any of their deeds.
> Because of this will not the land quake
> And everyone who dwells in it mourn?" (Amos 8:4-8)

It was this sin, along with others, that brought about the judgment of Israel when God sent the Assyrians to destroy them. In the time of Zephaniah, God would send the Babylonians against Judah for the same sins.

All who see evil in the land and do nothing are also guilty (1:12, 13).

"12 It will come about at that time
That I will search Jerusalem with lamps,
And I will punish the men
Who are stagnant in spirit,
Who say in their hearts,
'The Lord will not do good or evil!'

"^{13} Moreover, their wealth will become plunder
And their houses desolate;
Yes, they will build houses but not inhabit them,
And plant vineyards but not drink their wine."

There is a humorous story told of two people at a church who were talking. One said, "I think the biggest problems in the church today are ignorance and apathy, what do you think?" His friend quickly responded, "I don't know and I don't care!" It is interesting that those two things directly describe the attitude of the people of God from both Israel and Judah. They had become ignorant of the Word of God and they simply didn't care. They are described as having become *"stagnant in spirit."* They had become complacent, didn't care about anything. They were not interested and God was not important to them. They said of Him, *"The Lord will not do good or evil!" (1:12).* They didn't think He cared and they didn't care either.

When a person turns away from God, that person also turns away from joy and purpose in life. When nothing has a purpose, what is the use of doing anything? They just watch and sit around like a stagnant pond that has no inflow of life-giving water. In a river, dead things go downstream. It takes effort to fight the current but it is the only way to get to the mountain heights where the water is pure. The people of Judah were stagnant, visionless, purposeless.

They must have thought that they could hide from God, the all-knowing and ever-present One. God will find them. He will search every hiding place in Jerusalem with lamps. No one can hide from the piercing all-seeing eyes of the Almighty.

> **"'Can a man hide himself in hiding places
> So I do not see him?' declares the Lord.
> 'Do I not fill the heavens and the earth?' declares the
> Lord."** (Jeremiah 23:24)

The complacent, or stagnant ones had become wealthy through dishonest practices and all that they had accumulated was about to become the plunder of the Babylonians (1:13). The vineyards they owned would become wine for the enemy (1:13).

> **"For My eyes are on all their ways; they are not hidden from My face, nor is their iniquity concealed from My eyes."** (Jeremiah 16:17)

The Babylonian invasion is described (1:14-18).

[14] Near is the great day of the LORD,
Near and coming very quickly;
Listen, the day of the LORD!
In it the warrior cries out bitterly.
[15] A day of wrath is that day,
A day of trouble and distress,
A day of destruction and desolation,
A day of darkness and gloom,
A day of clouds and thick darkness,
[16] A day of trumpet and battle cry
Against the fortified cities
And the high corner towers.
[17] I will bring distress on men
So that they will walk like the blind,
Because they have sinned against the LORD;
And their blood will be poured out like dust
And their flesh like dung.
[18] Neither their silver nor their gold
Will be able to deliver them
On the day of the LORD'S WRATH;
And all the earth will be devoured

In the fire of His jealousy,
For He will make a complete end,
Indeed a terrifying one,
Of all the inhabitants of the earth.

In Zephaniah's poetic fashion, he described the coming invasion and destruction that Babylon would bring against Judah. You can almost smell the smoke of battle and hear the screams of the people. It would be massive destruction and annihilation. It would also serve as a picture of the end of the age when the King of Glory returns and slays the enemies of Israel at the battle of Armageddon. It is referred to as "the Great Day of the Lord." This is the day when God gets His final word.

> "The day of the Lord is the day of His self-revelation to judge evil and bring His work of redemption among men to completion. On the one side His revelation of Himself fills men with terror and anguish, on the other side it is the cause of universal gladness, for the oppressions under which the world groaned come to an end and the reign of God begins: "The Lord is King! let the earth rejoice, let the multitude of the isles be glad ... for he cometh to rule the earth; he shall rule the world with righteousness, and the peoples with equity" (Psalm 97:1; Psalm 98:9)
> (Cambridge Bible School)

A LIST OF THE CONSEQUENCES OF THE GREAT DAY OF THE LORD (1:15-18).

- Bitter weeping of the conquered armies. (1:14)
- Trouble and distress of the people. (1:15)
- Destruction and desolation of the land. (1:15)
- Darkness and fear cover the land. (1:15)
- Fortified cities would fall at the terrifying sound of enemy trumpets. (1:16)
- Confusion would spread and people stumble around like blind men. (1:17)

- Blood runs in the streets and covers them like the dust of the earth. (1:17)
- The flesh of the conquered rots and the stench is like dung. (1:17)
- All the things men trusted in fail them on that day. (1:18)
- The Holy jealousy of God against sin is satisfied. (1:18)
- God makes a complete end of all evil on the earth. (1:18)

When the last battles on earth take place in the final fulfillment of the Great day of the Lord, the destruction of all enemies of God will be complete. Here is one of several descriptions from Revelation of that great day:

> **"So the angel swung his sickle to the earth and gathered the clusters from the vine of the earth, and threw them into the great wine press of the wrath of God. And the wine press was trodden outside the city, and blood came out from the wine press, up to the horses' bridles, for a distance of two hundred miles."** (Revelation 14:19, 20)

This description in verses 1:14-18 has a dual fulfillment. The Babylonian invasion was close at hand. It would be *"A day of trumpet and battle cry against the fortified cities And the high corner towers"* (1:16). As you continue to read through the verses it shifts to a larger picture of the Great Day of the Lord when *"all the earth will be devoured in the fire of His jealousy, For He will make a complete end, Indeed a terrifying one, of all the inhabitants of the earth"* (1:18).

Zephaniah Two

WOE ORACLES AGAINST JUDAH'S ENEMIES.

In chapter one, God brought scathing charges against Judah for its many sins. Chapter two begins with one more appeal for Judah to repent. Then, God tells the enemy nations of Judah what will happen to them. He singled out the Philistines, Moabites, Ammonites, Ethiopians, and the Assyrians.

A final call to Judah to repent (2:1-3).

¹ Gather yourselves together, yes, gather,
O nation without shame,
² Before the decree takes effect—
The day passes like the chaff—
Before the burning anger of the LORD comes upon you,
Before the day of the LORD's anger comes upon you.
³ Seek the LORD,
All you humble of the earth
Who have carried out His ordinances;
Seek righteousness, seek humility.
Perhaps you will be hidden
In the day of the LORD's anger.

This is a final appeal to Judah; a nation God describes as without shame (2:1). He reminds them of His decree for Babylon to invade and destroy them. It is time, God tells them, to come together as a people and seriously consider one final chance to repent of their sins and seek the Lord. The day will soon come upon them when they will be burned up like the leftover hulls of the wheat harvest, the chaff (2:2). When dry chaff is burned it is consumed quickly, a very visual image the people of Judah all understood well. But, if they would seek the Lord while He may be found, perhaps His burning anger can be avoided (2:2).

Then he appealed particularly to the *"humble of the earth."* These are the remnant of Judah who have not followed after false gods and have kept God's laws and sacrificed to the true Lord. They had not acted arrogantly like their fallen brothers. They were being encouraged to stay true, seek righteousness and God might shield them from the horror to come. They might find a hiding place in their Savior. It was not a guarantee of escape from the Babylonians, but it was a hope. Believing in God is not a promise that any child of God will escape earthly trials but we still ask God for His mercy. That is what He was saying to His remnant.

Woe to the Philistines (2:4-7).

4 For Gaza will be abandoned
And Ashkelon a desolation;
Ashdod will be driven out at noon
And Ekron will be uprooted.
5 Woe to the inhabitants of the seacoast,
The nation of the Cherethites!
The word of the LORD is against you,
O Canaan, land of the Philistines;
And I will destroy you
So that there will be no inhabitant.
6 So the seacoast will be pastures,
With caves for shepherds and folds for flocks.
7 And the coast will be
For the remnant of the house of Judah,
They will pasture on it.
In the houses of Ashkelon they will lie down at evening;

For the LORD their God will care for them
And restore their fortune.

THE PHILISTINES.

The Philistines had a long history of fighting against Judah. They formed alliances with the major enemies of the people of God. They were a nation of war. Very little is known about them culturally since they left no written records like other cultures. When they are mentioned by other nations it is about facing them in battle. War seemed to be their life. Goliath was a Philistine. In 1 Samuel 17, we read how a young shepherd boy, David, killed the mighty giant the Philistines used to taunt Israel. David went from an unknown boy to become king over Israel. His victory over the warring Philistines began his path to the crown. David's exploits are legendary and they began with his faith in God and the defeat of the mighty Philistine's army.

A "Philistine" is sometimes used to describe someone who is warlike or who doesn't appreciate art or culture."
(Live Science.com)

The pagan Philistines continued to be a warring people for 400 years after their defeat in the days of Saul and David. They always hated Israel and conspired with other nations for centuries to overthrow the people of God. Zephaniah proclaimed a warning to the Philistines that their final destruction was at hand. The same Babylonians that God used to discipline His people, Judah, would destroy the Philistines as well. The land the Philistines held would one day be taken over by the remnant of Judah. The Philistines are no longer seen in written history after the destruction of the region by the Babylonian King Nebuchadnezzar II. He conquered several Philistine cities, including Ashkelon.

A word to the Philistines living on Crete (2:5-7).

"5 Woe to the inhabitants of the seacoast,
The nation of the Cherethites!
The word of the Lord is against you,
O Canaan, land of the Philistines;
And I will destroy you
So that there will be no inhabitant.
6 So the seacoast will be pastures,
With caves for shepherds and folds for flocks.
7 And the coast will be
For the remnant of the house of Judah," (2:5-7)

The "Cherethites"(2:5), according to archeologists, were a colony of Philistines that inhabited the island of Crete. They introduced bows and arrows to the Cretans. The Philistines were known mostly for their warfare.

According to 2 Samuel 8:18, the Cherethites were under Benaiah, the main enforcer, and assassin in David's mighty men. The "mighty men" were David's toughest military troop. When King David wanted someone executed, he often called on Benaiah. The Cherethites have been described by some as mercenaries, hired warriors to do battle.

> **"Benaiah the son of Jehoiada was over the Cherethites and the Pelethites; and David's sons were chief ministers."** (2 Samuel 8:18)

The word of the Lord was clear, all Philistines, including the Cherethites, were to be destroyed. They were pagan enemies of Judah and God was against them. It happened as God said it would. Today, there are no Philistines. They disappeared as an ethnic group in the 6th century B.C. according to historical records.

But before we leave this story, we do have the Bible to shed light on Israel and the Philistines.

A BRIEF SUMMARY WHAT WE KNOW OF THE PHILISTINES IN THE BOOKS OF JUDGES AND 1 SAMUEL.

- Before the Kings of Israel, Judges ruled the land that God had given His people.
- The Philistines were an ancient warring people who inhabited the coastline of what we today know is part of the land of Israel.
- The primary god of the Philistines was Dagon. Dagon was a Mesopotamian/Canaanite god of fertility, usually depicted as a fish god. Large temples were built in honor of this false god.
- There was continual war between Israel and the Philistines.
- God raised a man named Sampson who became a judge over Israel. The parents of Sampson were told by God, "*He*

will begin to save Israel from the hands of the Philistines." (Judges 13:5)

- Sampson had numerous conflicts with the Philistines and killed many. He was filled with special strength to war against the Philistines.
- Sampson was a man, strong in body, but weak in morals and wisdom.
- Against his family's counsel, Samson lusted after and married a Philistine woman from Timnah. She was a pagan worshipper of Dagon. Through a series of deceits and intrigues, Sampson lost his new wife, his friends, his shaky relationship with the Philistines and ended up killing many of the Philistines in anger.
- More killings and battles followed. The Philistines wanted to capture Sampson but he kept killing them. Israel was angry with him for stirring up the hostility of the Philistines against them. Sampson was a judge over the land for 20 years after that.
- Sampson fell in love with another Philistine named Delilah. The Philistines used Sampson's weakness of his flesh when they got Delilah to cause him to break his vows and lose God's presence and his strength. Sampson was blinded, mocked, and imprisoned.
- God later restored the strength of Sampson during a festival in the temple of Dagon. Sampson destroyed the temple and died with the Philistines.
- The last of the Judges was a good judge named Samuel. He was the one to anoint Saul to be the first king of Israel.
- The Philistines and Israel had a battle and Israel lost many men. They felt they lost this battle because God was not with them (1 Samuel 4). They made a bad decision. They took the Ark of the Covenant out of the Tabernacle and carried it to the battlefield believing God's presence was with them. But God was not with them.

- The Philistines killed 30,000 Israelites, captured the Ark and placed it in a temple of Dagon. When word of this defeat reached Eli the priest that his sons were also killed, He fell over dead. His daughter-in-law prematurely gave birth to a son whom they named Ichabod which means *"the Glory of God has departed from Israel."*
- The presence of the Ark in the temple of Dagon brought a series of curses and calamities upon the Philistines. It was so bad they begged Israel to take the Ark back.

The story of what happened when the Philistines captured the Ark of the Covenant is definitely worth reading.

> **"Now the hand of the LORD WAS HEAVY ON THE ASHDODITES, AND HE MADE THEM FEEL DEVASTATED AND STRUCK THEM WITH TUMORS,** *both* **Ashdod and its territories. When the men of Ashdod saw that it was so, they said, 'The ark of the God of Israel must not remain with us, because His hand is severe on us and on Dagon our god.' So they sent** *word* **and gathered all the governors of the Philistines to them, and said, 'What shall we do with the ark of the God of Israel?' And they said, 'Have the ark of the God of Israel brought to Gath.' So they took the ark of the God of Israel away.**

> **After they had taken it away, the hand of the LORD WAS AGAINST THE CITY,** *creating* **a very great panic; and He struck the people of the city, from the young to the old, so that tumors broke out on them. So they sent the ark of God to Ekron. And as the ark of God came to Ekron, the Ekronites cried out, saying, 'They have brought the ark of the God of Israel to us, to kill us and our people!' Therefore they sent** *word* **and gathered all the governors of the Philistines, and said, 'Send away the ark of the God of Israel and let it return to its own place, so that it will not kill us and our people!' For there was a deadly panic throughout the city; the hand of God was very heavy there.**

And the people who did not die were struck with tumors, and the outcry of the city went up to heaven."
(1 Samuel 5:6-12)

This is Dagon, the fish god of the Philistines.

Although there are many more stories to tell, this gives us some background to understand the anger of God toward the Philistines. Zephaniah was given the task to tell the Philistines that the patience of God had run out.

The Philistines never understood that Israel was not their ultimate enemy. Their enemy was God.

> **"Woe to the inhabitants of the seacoast,**
> **The nation of the Cherethites!**
> **The word of the Lord is against you,"** (2:5)

APPLICATION.

When we read the stories of Israel and the Philistines, we almost end up shaking our heads. Did anyone learn any lessons? Did you ever button up a shirt or sweater and you got the first button wrong? The longer you kept going the worse it became. No matter when you realize your mistake you still have to undo what you have done. The sooner you do it the better. We must never forget the first button in the moral law of God. If we get that one wrong, everything from then on is wrong and it gets worse for us the longer we continue where we are going. Here is the first button:

> *"Then God spoke all these words, saying,* "I am the LORD your God, who brought you out of the land of Egypt, out of the house of slavery.
>
> "You shall have no other gods before Me. "You shall not make for yourself an idol, or any likeness of what is in heaven above or on the earth beneath, or in the water under the earth. You shall not worship them nor serve them; for I, the Lord your God, am a jealous God, inflicting the punishment of the fathers on the children, on the third and the fourth generations of those who hate Me, but showing favor to thousands, to those who love Me and keep My commandments." (Exodus 20:1-6)

Now think of this story again. God delivered His people from slavery. He is a loving God but He is also Holy. He alone deserves our worship and promises blessing upon all who love Him. He has demonstrated in all that He has done that this is true. God still honors all who follow Him and love Him. What He asks is simple. We are not supposed to go out in our gardens and dig up rocks, paint ugly faces on them, and then bow down and worship them.

What a contrast. We believe in the God who loved the lost so much He sent His only Son to pay the penalty for our sins. The pagans believe in gods of carved wood, donkey bones, and piles of animal manure that people spread on their faces while going blind staring at the sun? Has Satan so blinded the minds of people that do these things? Do they honestly believe the lie? Yes! While Moses was on Mount Sinai getting the Law, his brother, Aaron, was making a golden calf at the base of the mountain for the people. Yes, Aaron and the people who just watched the Red Sea part and God provide all they needed in the wilderness, wanted a god of gold.

So, what is the application? When we don't remain faithful to the Word of God, we lose touch with the God of the Word. The more we learn of God, the more we love God. If we will stay committed to the Lord, we will never hear the words Zephaniah had to deliver to the Philistines, *"The word of the Lord is against you."*

Woe to the Moabites and Ammonites (2:8-11).

8 "I have heard the taunting of Moab
And the revilings of the sons of Ammon,
With which they have taunted My people
And become arrogant against their territory.
9 "Therefore, as I live," declares the LORD of hosts,
The God of Israel,
"Surely Moab will be like Sodom
And the sons of Ammon like Gomorrah—
A place possessed by nettles and salt pits,
And a perpetual desolation.
The remnant of My people will plunder them
And the remainder of My nation will inherit them."

¹⁰ This they will have in return for their pride, because they have taunted and become arrogant against the people of the LORD of hosts. ¹¹ The LORD will be terrifying to them, for He will starve all the gods of the earth; and all the coastlands of the nations will bow down to Him, everyone from his *own* place.

WHO WERE THE MOABITES AND AMMONITES?

Moab and Ammon were ungodly sons of Lot through an incestual relationship with his daughters after the destruction of Sodom and Gomorrah.

> **"Thus, both the daughters of Lot were with child by their father. The firstborn bore a son, and called his name Moab; he is the father of the Moabites to this day. As for the younger, she also bore a son, and called his name Ben-ammi; he is the father of the sons of Ammon to this day."** (Genesis 19:37, 38)

Lot's family came out of Sodom and Gomorrah. Lot's wife never wanted to leave and looked back to see the destruction of her beloved home. She died there and never looked at anything else again. From what we know of Lot and his daughters, they left

Sodom but Sodom never left them. The nations that came from them were filled with pagan idolatry.

The Moabites settled east of the Dead Sea. The Ammonites chose the land north of Moab.

Even though there was a family connection of the Moabites and Ammonites to Abraham, the children born of Lot chose to follow a different path than the God of Abraham. They became idolaters. They influenced the children of Abraham to follow Baal worship on its way into Canaan (Num. 25:1–3). Both the Ammonites and the Moabites were the ones that hired Balaam to curse Israel and were thus not allowed to enter the Lord's family line (Deut. 23:3–4). One of Moab's famous converts to faith was Ruth, the Moabitess, who renounced the god Moloch and believed in the God of Abraham, Isaac, and Jacob. She is listed in the line of David, and hence, the Messiah.

The Moabites practiced child sacrifices to their false god Moloch.

Because of idolatry and the hostility to God's children, the lines of Moab and Ammon invited the wrath of God. They were cursed with a permanent desolation (2:9). The false gods would be brought low as well and exposed as false before the world. The lands of Moab and Ammon would become desolate like the towns their father left, Sodom and Gomorrah. Salt pits and stinging nettles were all that would remain (2:9). Their destruction was brought about by the Babylonian invasion just like the destruction of the Philistines.

Their arrogant mocking of the true sons of God would turn to terror in the presence of God (2:10, 11). The land would one day be in Israel's possession and all peoples will bow down to the Lord (2:9, 11).

Woe to the Ethiopians (2:12).

¹²"You also, O Ethiopians, will be slain by My sword."

WHY WAS GOD ANGRY WITH ETHIOPIA IN NORTH AFRICA?

"Now (King)Asa had an army of 300,000 from Judah, bearing large shields and spears, and 280,000 from Benjamin, bearing shields and wielding bows; all of them were valiant warriors.

Now Zerah the Ethiopian came out against them with an army of a million men and 300 chariots, and he came to Mareshah. So Asa went out to meet him, and they drew up in battle formation in the valley of Zephathah at Mareshah. Then Asa called to the LORD HIS GOD AND SAID, "LORD, THERE IS NO ONE BESIDES YOU TO HELP *in the battle* between the powerful and those who have no strength; so help us, O LORD our God, for we trust in You, and in Your name have come against this multitude. O Lord, You are our God; let not man prevail against You."

So the LORD routed the Ethiopians before Asa and before Judah, and the Ethiopians fled. Asa and the people who *were* with him pursued them as far as Gerar; and so many Ethiopians fell that they could not recover, for they were shattered before the LORD AND BEFORE HIS ARMY."
(2 CHRONICLES 14:8-13)

The Babylonians would later overrun and finish off the remainder of the Ethiopians when they invaded Ammon and Moab. It is interesting that when the Babylonians slaughtered the Ethiopians with the sword, God refers to it as *My sword.* He is at all times the Sovereign and in control. The prophet Habakkuk struggled with the thought of God using the Babylonians to discipline Judah, His people. God told Habakkuk that He, the Sovereign of all nations, would bring the wicked Babylonians to judgment. He used them as His instrument to discipline Judah and punish her enemies which included Ethiopia.

Note: For an expanded explanation of this, read the commentary on the Book of Habakkuk in this volume.

Woe to the Assyrians (2:13-15).

13 And He will stretch out His hand against the north
And destroy Assyria,
And He will make Nineveh a desolation,
Parched like the wilderness.
14 Flocks will lie down in her midst,
All beasts which range in herds;
Both the pelican and the hedgehog
Will lodge in the tops of her pillars;
Birds will sing in the window,
Desolation *will be* on the threshold;
For He has laid bare the cedar work.
15 This is the exultant city
Which dwells securely,
Who says in her heart,
"I am, and there is no one besides me."
How she has become a desolation,

A resting place for beasts!
Everyone who passes by her will hiss
And wave his hand *in contempt.*

Reading Zephaniah is like attending a parade of wickedness. They march in one after another and just when you think the parade is over, an even more wicked nation appears. This is the final participant in the parade, Assyria. It was one of the largest and most evil empires in the world. So, what ended their reign of terror? Another empire of course. The Medo-Babylonian empire brought them down when they seized Nineveh, the capital city of the Assyrians in 612 B.C. They never grew back to strength after that fatal blow.

> **"And He will stretch out His hand against the north**
> **And destroy Assyria,**
> **And He will make Nineveh a desolation,**
> **Parched like the wilderness."** (2:13)

This is the "great city" of Nineveh today.

Assyria was a powerful nation that felt they were invincible, *"This is the exultant city which dwells securely, who says in her heart, "I am, and there is no one besides me." (*2:15). As we know, God resists the proud and gives grace to the lowly, the humble (James 4:6). Jesus told His crowds the same thing, *"Whoever exalts himself shall be humbled; and whoever humbles himself shall be exalted"* (Matthew 23:12). God appealed to Judah to humble themselves and repent for this reason. But for Assyria, their day of glory was over.

> **"This is the exultant city**
> **Which dwells securely,**
> **Who says in her heart,**
> **'I am, and there is no one besides me.'"** (2:15)

As God predicted, today the region is sand and piles of rubble. It has been 2,600 years since the fall of Nineveh and it has never been rebuilt.

> **"How she has become a desolation,**
> **A resting place for beasts!**
> **Everyone who passes by her will hiss**
> **And wave his hand in contempt."** (2:15)

Note: For more information on the demise of Assyria and Babylon, see the commentaries on Jonah and Nahum. Zephaniah shows us that all nations and empires are used by God for His purpose. He is the Sovereign over all the nations.

The next chapter continues God's woe call. The judgments focus on the sins of Jerusalem's leadership, both political and spiritual.

Zephaniah Three

Woe to defiled Jerusalem and her leaders (3:1-4).

¹ Woe to her who is rebellious and defiled,
The tyrannical city!
² She heeded no voice,
She accepted no instruction.
She did not trust in the LORD,
She did not draw near to her God.
³ Her princes within her are roaring lions,
Her judges are wolves at evening;
They leave nothing for the morning.
⁴ Her prophets are reckless, treacherous men;
Her priests have profaned the sanctuary.
They have done violence to the law.

This chapter covers the full range of God's wrath against the sins of Jerusalem to the final exaltation of the remnant in the great day of the Lord. It goes from darkness to a bright light of hope.

We begin with the darkness. In his book, Amos warned the deceived people of Israel that they should not be looking for the Day of the Lord. He explained that they expected light but only darkness would be coming for them. And that is what happened when Assyria invaded. The people were looking for the fulfillment of the great promises of God for the children of Abraham. They mistakenly thought since they claimed the family line of

Abraham, it was a free ticket to blessing. Sadly, the nation had abandoned the Lord and His blessing was no longer upon them, only judgment remained.

Likewise, the people in the South expected Jerusalem to be the great city on the hill that would be the jewel of all nations. Zephaniah was sent by God to bring the word of the Lord to them and their city. This time God would send the Babylonians to be His instrument of discipline against His unfaithful people.

> **"Woe to her who is rebellious and defiled,**
> **The tyrannical city!**
> **She heeded no voice,**
> **She accepted no instruction.**
> **She did not trust in the Lord,**
> **She did not draw near to her God."** (3:1, 2)

How the mighty city had fallen, the city of David, the home of the greatest kings of the people of God. It is the most important city in the Bible and will one day be made new and become the capital of the new earth. But it has had a lot of dark days. Here is what Jesus said one day as he approached Jerusalem with His disciples:

> **"O Jerusalem, Jerusalem, the city that kills the prophets**
> **and stones those who are sent to it! How often would I**
> **have gathered your children together as a hen gathers**
> **her brood under her wings, and you were not willing! See,**
> **your house is left to you desolate. For I tell you, you will**
> **not see me again, until you say, 'Blessed is he who comes**
> **in the name of the Lord.'"** (Matthew 23:37-39)

Just as the Jewish nation in the time of Christ had not been faithful in God's Word, so it has had a similar history throughout time. They were seasonal. They fluctuated between seasons of repentance, restoration, and blessing with seasons of falling away into idolatry, corruption, and abuses of the poor and downtrodden. Zephaniah ministered in this last season.

In God's eyes, the oppressing enemy was Jerusalem, not Babylon. The sins of the nation were so great God called them the "*tyrannical city*," the city of oppression (3:1). The people did not listen to God, obey God, trust God, or draw near to God (3:2).

The weight of the sin of Jerusalem was mostly charged against those in leadership, the king, princes, priests, and prophets. That is who Zephaniah addresses:

> **"Her princes within her are roaring lions,**
> **Her judges are wolves at evening;**
> **They leave nothing for the morning.**
> **Her prophets are reckless, treacherous men;**
> **Her priests have profaned the sanctuary.**
> **They have done violence to the law."** (3:3, 4)

The princes, sons of the king, were often the worst of the leaders, even when kings were good kings. Judah had 19 kings in their history, only eight were followers of God. But their children did not always follow the faith of the good fathers. Zephaniah describes them as powerful lions but destructive beasts against the powerless people of the land. The Judges were corrupted wolves taking advantage of their power and consuming the flock that trusted them. The prophets were the same. The ones that should be speaking the truth were treacherous men who destroyed faith. The priests were not holy but profane, sinful servants who served only themselves. The very law they were entrusted with was ignored and violated. The entire nation was in a dreadful condition.

TO SUMMARIZE.

The leaders didn't lead, the judges didn't judge, the prophets didn't speak the truth and the priests didn't serve the Temple or honor the sacrifices. Every office God had established failed the people.

The Lord is righteous (3:5-7).

5 The LORD is righteous within her;
He will do no injustice.
Every morning He brings His justice to light;
He does not fail.
But the unjust knows no shame.
6 "I have cut off nations;
Their corner towers are in ruins.
I have made their streets desolate,
With no one passing by;
Their cities are laid waste,
Without a man, without an inhabitant.
7 "I said, 'Surely you will revere Me,
Accept instruction.'
So her dwelling will not be cut off
According to all that I have appointed concerning her.
But they were eager to corrupt all their deeds.

It is refreshing to see the purity and righteousness of God after looking at the horrid condition of Jerusalem. The princes, judges, and priests had all failed but God is by nature Just and can do no injustice.

> **"The Lord is righteous within her;**
> **He will do no injustice.**
> **Every morning He brings His justice to light;**
> **He does not fail.**
> **But the unjust knows no shame."** (3:5)

God, being Just, must punish sin and all injustice. God reminded the people that He is a God who disposes of nations, so nothing is too difficult for Him. Cities that were filled with people have been turned into wastelands at His hand. Jerusalem should heed the warning that the same would happen to them if they ignore Him.

"I have cut off nations;
Their corner towers are in ruins.
I have made their streets desolate,
With no one passing by;
Their cities are laid waste,
Without a man, without an inhabitant." (3:6)

What was the response of the people who, of all people, knew what God could do?

"I said, 'Surely you will revere Me,
Accept instruction.'
So her dwelling will not be cut off
According to all that I have appointed concerning her.
But they were eager to corrupt all their deeds." (3:7)

After all the warnings, the time for judgment had come. The people chose to be on the wrong side of His justice. They didn't just choose to sin over obeying God, they did it eagerly, they gladly rushed into it (3:7).

The future hope of Jerusalem (3:8-11).

8 "Therefore wait for Me," declares the LORD,
"For the day when I rise up as a witness.
Indeed, My decision is to gather nations,
To assemble kingdoms,
To pour out on them My indignation,
All My burning anger;
For all the earth will be devoured
By the fire of My zeal.
9 "For then I will give to the peoples purified lips,
That all of them may call on the name of the LORD,
To serve Him shoulder to shoulder.
10 "From beyond the rivers of Ethiopia
My worshipers, My dispersed ones,

Will bring My offerings.
¹¹ "In that day you will feel no shame
Because of all your deeds
By which you have rebelled against Me;
For then I will remove from your midst
Your proud, exulting ones,
And you will never again be haughty
On My holy mountain.

A common pattern found in the messages of many of the prophets was to first list the offenses of the people of God and/or the enemy nations of Israel and then to finish with the hope of a restored Israel. Two clear facts come from this. First, Israel abandoned God to serve idols. As a nation, they greatly offended God and brought his righteous wrath upon themselves. Second, God is faithful to his promises and covenants. There has and always will remain a faithful remnant of true believers through even the worst of times. These are true Israel. In the end times, there will be a great restoration of Israel. They will get their land back and will be desired by the nations as friends of God.

The book of Zephaniah has come to the restoration section of his book. We will be transported to the times of the end when Jesus will reign on the earth for 1,000 years. The Millennium marks the end of the rule of the evil nations on the earth. King Jesus will be on the throne. Israel will finally be back in their God-given land and never leave it again.

Zephaniah begins with the prophecy of God's wrath poured out on the enemy nations of Israel:

> "'Therefore wait for Me,' declares the Lord,
> 'For the day when I rise up as a witness.
> Indeed, My decision is to gather nations,
> To assemble kingdoms,

To pour out on them My indignation,
All My burning anger;
For all the earth will be devoured
By the fire of My zeal.'" (3:8)

The Millennium comes at the end of the age. The Great Tribulation on the earth will be over, the battle of Armageddon will be ended by the second coming of Christ. Jesus will then take His rightful place as the King of kings and Lord of lords over the earth. The judgment of the nations takes place at that time as well. All those who cursed Israel will feel the consequences of the Abrahamic Covenant. They will be cursed. God will assemble all the enemy nations and dispense His holy justice on them. All the earth will be consumed by the fire of God's holy wrath. Israel, who has been tormented and mocked by these kingdoms over the centuries, will finally be vindicated. Zephaniah told the people in his day that God's word to His remnant was *"'Therefore wait for Me,' declares the Lord, 'For the day when I rise up as a witness.'"* (3:8). Hard days were certainly ahead but he wanted the faithful to not lose heart.

The next thing that happens after the judgment of the nations is the consecration and purification of His people.

> **"For then I will give to the peoples purified lips,**
> **That all of them may call on the name of the Lord,**
> **To serve Him shoulder to shoulder."** (3:9)

This marks the end of all wars. "Peace on earth and goodwill to man" will be more than a popular song.

> **"And He will judge between the nations, and will render**
> **decisions for many peoples; And they will hammer their**
> **swords into plowshares and their spears into pruning**
> **hooks. Nation will not lift up sword against nation, And**
> **never again will they learn war."** (Isaiah 2:4)

Since the world will work side by side *"To serve Him shoulder to shoulder"* (3:9), some think there will be a common language again on the earth as it was before the confusion of the languages at the tower of Babel (Genesis 11).

> **"Most Bible scholars see this as fulfilled in the days of the Millennium when Jesus reigns for 1,000 years over this earth after His return in power and glory. From this passage, many scholars believe that in that day the world will go back to a common language – perhaps Hebrew."** (David Guzik)

An interesting phrase is used by God which has a very special meaning to the Jewish people. He says, *"For then I will give to the peoples purified lips."*

The prophet Isaiah had described the nation as a people of unclean lips so to see the day coming when they will have purified lips had to be a wonderful hope. God had not given up on them. The day of the ultimate fulfillment of Isaiah's vision will come about on that day.

> **"In the year of King Uzziah's death I saw the Lord sitting on a throne, lofty and exalted, with the train of His robe filling the temple. Seraphim stood above Him, each having six wings: with two he covered his face, and with two he covered his feet, and with two he flew. And one called out to another and said,**
> > **'Holy, Holy, Holy, is the LORD OF HOSTS,**
> > **The whole earth is full of His glory.'**
> **And the foundations of the thresholds trembled at the voice of him who called out, while the temple was filling with smoke. Then I said,**
> > **'Woe is me, for I am ruined!**
> > **Because I am a man of unclean lips,**
> > **And I live among a people of unclean lips;**
> > **For my eyes have seen the King, the LORD OF HOSTS.'**
> **Then one of the seraphim flew to me with a burning coal in his hand, which he had taken from the altar with tongs.**

> He touched my mouth with it and said, 'Behold, this has touched your lips; and your iniquity is taken away and your sin is forgiven.'" (Isaiah 6:1-7)

The restored Jewish nation will come back to Jerusalem to worship again. They will come from the ends of the earth, from *"beyond the rivers of Ethiopia (3:10).* The years of the rebellion of Israel will be forgiven and shame removed. Never again will the arrogant inhabit the kingdom of their God. Verses 10 and 11 describe this wonderful day.

> "From beyond the rivers of Ethiopia
> My worshipers, My dispersed ones,
> Will bring My offerings.
> In that day you will feel no shame
> Because of all your deeds
> By which you have rebelled against Me;
> For then I will remove from your midst
> Your proud, exulting ones,
> And you will never again be haughty
> On My holy mountain." (3:10, 11)

A song of the Remnant of Israel in a restored Jerusalem (3:12-20).

12 "But I will leave among you
A humble and lowly people,
And they will take refuge in the name of the LORD.
13 "The remnant of Israel will do no wrong
And tell no lies,
Nor will a deceitful tongue
Be found in their mouths;
For they will feed and lie down
With no one to make them tremble

14 Shout for joy, O daughter of Zion!
Shout *in triumph*, O Israel!

Rejoice and exult with all *your* heart,
O daughter of Jerusalem!
¹⁵ The LORD HAS TAKEN AWAY *His* judgments against you,
He has cleared away your enemies.
The King of Israel, the LORD, IS IN YOUR MIDST;
You will fear disaster no more.
¹⁶ In that day it will be said to Jerusalem:
"Do not be afraid, O Zion;
Do not let your hands fall limp.
¹⁷ "The LORD YOUR GOD IS IN YOUR MIDST,
A victorious warrior.
He will exult over you with joy,
He will be quiet in His love,
He will rejoice over you with shouts of joy.
¹⁸ "I will gather those who grieve about the appointed feasts—
They came from you, *O Zion*;
The reproach *of exile* is a burden on them.
¹⁹ "Behold, I am going to deal at that time
With all your oppressors,
I will save the lame
And gather the outcast,
And I will turn their shame into praise and renown
In all the earth.
²⁰ "At that time I will bring you in,
Even at the time when I gather you together;
Indeed, I will give you renown and praise
Among all the peoples of the earth,
When I restore your fortunes before your eyes,"
Says the LORD.

If you had to pick one verse out of this amazing song of restoration and joy, it might be verse 17.

> "The Lord your God is in your midst,
> A victorious warrior.
> He will exult over you with joy,
> He will be quiet in His love,
> He will rejoice over you with shouts of joy." (3:17)

After a long and difficult journey, God's prodigal children will come home. God will cover their sins and throw a great banquet for them and sing to them and shout for joy. Imagine, God will shout for Joy! He returned to earth with a shout and now He is rejoicing to have His children safely home at last. **Note:** The Hebrew word translated "shout" can also mean "sing." He will rejoice over His people with singing. Here is that same Hebrew word used by Isaiah to describe that great day:

> "Sing, O ye heavens; for the LORD hath done it: shout, ye lower parts of the earth: break forth into singing, ye mountains, O forest, and every tree therein: for the LORD hath redeemed Jacob, and glorified himself in Israel."
> (Isaiah 44:23)

The English preacher, Spurgeon, was thrilled to think about this event:

> "Think of the great Jehovah singing! Can you imagine it? Is it possible to conceive of the Deity breaking into a song: Father, Son, and Holy Ghost together singing over the redeemed? God is so happy in the love which he bears to his people that he breaks the eternal silence, and sun and moon and stars with astonishment hear God chanting a hymn of joy." (Charles Spurgeon)

AN IMMENSE THOUGHT.

Can you even picture what this verse is saying? We spend our days in a world of noise. Empty, worldly music bombards our minds. But one day . . . one day, the universe will tremble when God sings to His prodigal children who are all finally home safe. The stars will shake, the moon will dance, the galaxies will hear the joy of God flooding every square inch of the infinite universe. The ever-present, all-powerful, all-loving, all-holy One will release His infinite glory in a song for His children. God is going to sing for us.

> **"The Lord your God is in your midst,**
> **A victorious warrior.**
> **He will exult over you with joy,**
> **He will be quiet in His love,**
> **He will rejoice over you with shouts (songs) of joy."** (3:17)

This final poetic song contains so many hopes and promises of God that one could fill up a book describing them. Let me simply list the blessings found in Zephaniah 3:12-20.

- God will change the heart of His people. (3:12)
- God will be Israel's final refuge, hiding place. (3:12)
- All lying and deception will be removed. (3:13)
- No more false prophets or lying tongues. (3:13)
- They will eat their meals in peace, with no fear of invaders. (3:13)
- Shouts of fear will be turned into shouts of joy. (3:14)
- Triumph will replace trials. (3:14)
- All enemies will be removed forever, all judgments are gone. (3:15)
- The King of Israel, the Messiah, will be in their midst. (3:15)
- The fear of coming disasters will be removed, peace will rule the land. (3:15)
- The people made weak by fear will be given strength by God. (3:16)
- God will sing for joy over His people. (3:17)
- God will be the warrior King and worshipped as such. (3:17)

- The long-lost feasts of Israel will be reinstituted as worship and celebration. (3:18)
- God will wipe away all the reproaches of the past. (3:18)
- Every oppressor of Israel will be dealt with at that time. (3:19)
- God will save the lame and the outcast and remove their shame. (3:19)
- God will give special honor to all who suffered in poverty previously. (3:19)
- All of God's chosen people will receive honor from the people of the earth. (3:20)
- God will restore all the fortunes of Israel, all those things lost over the years. (3:20)

In some ways, the story of Job has some similarities to the story of Israel. Job was a man of God, but in his life, he lost most things that he had accumulated, his family, his houses and lands, and his health. He faced confusion, mocking by some and trials kept coming his way. Like the remnant of Israel, he remained faithful to God even when others did not. At the end of Job's life, God restored the fortunes Job lost during his life.

> **"The Lord restored the fortunes of Job when he prayed for his friends, and the Lord increased all that Job had twofold. Then all his brothers and all his sisters and all who had known him before came to him, and they ate bread with him in his house; and they consoled him and comforted him for all the adversities that the Lord had brought on him. And each one gave him one piece of money, and each a ring of gold. The Lord blessed the latter days of Job more than his beginning; and he had 14,000 sheep and 6,000 camels and 1,000 yoke of oxen and 1,000 female donkeys. He had seven sons and three daughters. He named the first Jemimah, and the second Keziah, and the third Keren-happuch. In all the land no women were found so fair as Job's daughters; and their father gave**

them inheritance among their brothers. After this, Job lived 140 years, and saw his sons and his grandsons, four generations. And Job died, an old man and full of days." (Job 42:10-27)

God knows how to write the end of a story. He is writing the end of Israel's story. He is writing the end of our story. He is writing the end of all history. And then He will write the new story for all of us. I can't wait to see that one.

JOEL

The day of the locusts
and the Day of the LORD.

"It will come about
after this
That I will pour out
My Spirit on all
mankind;"

Joel 2:28

Introduction

What do we know about Joel?

To put it simply, we know almost nothing about the prophet Joel or when he wrote his book. It is one of the most mysterious books in the Bible. Peter quotes from it on the day of Pentecost and even that quotation can be very confusing. We will look at that later. The issue of interpretation must be addressed before we begin the study. This author has no question about the authenticity of the book but also accepts the fact that it is nearly impossible to explain everything in the book of Joel.

Interpretation problems with the book.

The big problem of interpreting the book of Joel comes from the uncertain dating of the book.

1. If one dates the book in the early days of the nation of Israel (800 B.C.), then the locusts which are described as an army in chapter two are referring to either the soon coming Assyrian invasion as Amos and Hosea prophesied, or it could be describing the more distant day of the Babylonian invasion, or even a Last Days event.

2. If the book of Joel is dated as just before the destruction of Jerusalem by the Babylonians in 586 B.C., then Joel was describing either the Babylonian army or a future army in the Last Days.

3. If the book of Joel is dated after the fall of Jerusalem, in the days of Ezra and Nehemiah, then the army referred to, in detail, is future and must be placed in the Last Days since nothing like it has happened in history. It could not be referring to Assyria or Babylon.

Good Bible commentators are all over the map on this issue since there is no way to verify when Joel wrote the prophecy.

One interesting factor is the large number of references which parallel the words of other prophets, most of which would not been alive if Joel lived in the early period. Did Jeremiah and Isaiah refer to Joel or did he refer to their writings?

Another issue is if the locusts of chapter two are referring to insects like the locusts in chapter one as some say, then why describe them in military terms in such detail? Those who choose to say it was all symbolic run into all kinds of problems stretching the texts to make insects appear as chariot wheels bouncing down cobblestone roads with flashing swords and lanterns. The question is why would Joel describe them as ferocious bugs in chapter one and then the same insects in Chapter two as fearful invaders in military armament and ravaging homes like a military column instead of destroying vegetation as we see in chapter one? If a literal interpretation is taken, the army of chapter two is real and will invade shortly or in the distant future.

This commentary will take the middle dating period and the literal approach as the best path. Would good Bible scholars agree? Yes. Would good Bible scholars disagree? Yes. Is it probable that the interpretative problems with this fascinating book of Joel will remain a mystery? Yes. The root problem is we can't date the book with certainty.

Joel simple Outline.

I. The Day of the Locusts (Joel 1).

II. The Day of the Lord in the time of Joel (Joel 2).

III. The Great Day of the Lord will come (Joel 3).

Joel One
THE DAY OF THE LOCUSTS

Pass it on! (1:1-3).

¹ The word of the LORD that came to Joel,
the son of Pethuel:

² Hear this, O elders,
And listen, all inhabitants of the land.
Has *anything like* this happened in your days
Or in your fathers' days?
³ Tell your sons about it,
And *let* your sons *tell* their sons,
And their sons the next generation.

Something big had happened to the land of Judah, not even the previous generations had witnessed. For the first two chapters, Joel described that event, how widespread it was, and why it happened. The lessons to be learned from it were so important that he wanted the parents to be sure the children knew what had taken place and what would happenen the days ahead.

> "These words, which I am commanding you today, shall be on your heart. And you shall repeat them diligently to your sons and speak of them when you sit in your house, when you walk on the road, when you lie down, and when you get up." (Deuteronomy 6:6, 7)

So, what was this amazing event that would be the central focus of Joel's book? It was a huge swarm of locusts sent to attack the land. Before we read what Joel said and how he related it to future events in the life of Judah, we need a short explanation of the size and destructive results of a locust swarm.

LOCUSTS.

"Locusts are the *swarming* phase of certain species of short-horned *grasshoppers.* These insects are usually solitary, but under certain circumstances become more abundant and change their behavior and habits and begin forming into large social groups and work cooperatively" (Wiki).

It is a mystery what causes this change. When overcrowding begins to occur, the insects have different appearances and behavior. Their color changes, they eat and breed, and become more of a social community rather than just individual grasshoppers.

The swarms they form become quite large. Some have grown into hundreds of square miles with densities of 200 million locusts per square mile. Billions upon billions of locusts fly across the land eating all vegetation in the path. Each locust will eat its weight in food every day.

A swarm of locusts can eat up to 400 million pounds of plants each day.

The swarm of locusts (1:4-7).

[4] What the gnawing locust has left, the swarming locust
has eaten;
And what the swarming locust has left, the creeping locust
has eaten;
And what the creeping locust has left, the stripping locust
has eaten.
[5] Awake, drunkards, and weep;
And wail, all you wine drinkers,
On account of the sweet wine
That is cut off from your mouth.
[6] For a nation has invaded my land,
Mighty and without number;
Its teeth are the teeth of a lion,
And it has the fangs of a lioness.
[7] It has made my vine a waste
And my fig tree splinters.
It has stripped them bare and cast *them* away;
Their branches have become white.

The first two chapters of Joel are filled with the images of a
locust swarm. The first image is an actual locust invasion that
decimated the land of Judah. The second image is a coming
military invasion that would sweep across the land and destroy
everything, like a locust swarm. We begin with an actual locust
swarm in chapter one. The images are given in vivid poetic
language.

The purpose of this account is to prepare the minds of Joel's
audience for the soon coming greater locust swarm when an
enemy army would sweep across the land and devour Judah.
Joel introduced the topic in the first verses when he said, *"listen,
all inhabitants of the land. Has anything like this happened in
your days?"* It doesn't matter if the locust swarm Joel describes

happened to the listeners or previously. They knew what locust swarms were and were aware of the massive devastation they caused. As we see in verse four, they were also aware of the different stages of the locust swarms.

> **What the gnawing locust has left, the swarming locust has eaten;**
> **And what the swarming locust has left, the creeping locust has eaten;**
> **And what the creeping locust has left, the stripping locust has eaten.** (1: 4)

Were these different types of locusts or phases or stages of the locust swarm dynamics?

> **"Four plagues had come upon the land: palmer worms, locusts, cankerworms, and caterpillars. Some of the best authorities on the locust, as well as Hebrew scholars, maintain that four stages of the development of the locust are described here. The context shows what they did to their fair land. The advance column destroyed every leaf and blade of grass. Those that followed even devoured the bark from the trees. The noise of their wings was heard for miles, and the land looked as though it had been swept by fire."** (Paul Van Gorder)

This is the pattern that swarms follow. So, was this a natural disaster that just happened, or was this sent by God? God describes the swarm as His "great army."

> **"Then I will make up to you for the years**
> **That the swarming locust has eaten,**
> **The creeping locust, the stripping locust, and the gnawing locust,**
> **My great army which I sent among you.** (2:25)

This physical swarm was an act of God. A foretaste of the greater locust swarm yet to come, also engineered by God. It was meant to be a wake-up call for Judah.

A wakeup call.

"Awake, drunkards, and weep;
And wail, all you wine drinkers,
On account of the sweet wine
That is cut off from your mouth.
For a nation has invaded my land,
Mighty and without number;
Its teeth are the teeth of a lion,
And it has the fangs of a lioness.
It has made my vine a waste
And my fig tree splinters.
It has stripped them bare and cast them away;
Their branches have become white." (1:5-7)

The nation of Judah had become a land of drunkards, not knowing what was going on around them. While they were sleeping off their lives of excess an enemy entered their land. The locusts destroyed the plants and vines. The wine they craved was taken away from them since the locusts destroyed the grapevines. It was a judgment against the destructive lifestyles of the people. God even takes time to describe the locusts and details of how they destroyed the vines. They had teeth like iron, splintering the stalks, and stripping the branches until not a green, living part remained (1:6, 7).

The people of Judah mourn over the destruction (1:8-12).

8 "Wail like a virgin girded with sackcloth
For the bridegroom of her youth.
9 The grain offering and the drink offering are cut off
From the house of the Lord.
The priests mourn,
The ministers of the Lord.

¹⁰ The field is ruined,
The land mourns;
For the grain is ruined,
The new wine dries up,
Fresh oil fails.
¹¹ Be ashamed, O farmers,
Wail, O vinedressers,
For the wheat and the barley;
Because the harvest of the field is destroyed.
¹² The vine dries up
And the fig tree fails;
The pomegranate, the palm also, and the apple tree,
All the trees of the field dry up.
Indeed, rejoicing dries up
From the sons of men."

The drunkards mourned. The priests now mourn. Their drink offerings are cut off since the wine is gone. The grain is gone also, so they have no grain offerings (1:9). They are like a newly wedded virgin wife who has just lost her husband (1:8). It is described as the land, the soil, and the spoiled wine all weeping (1:10).

The farmers also mourn because the land is ruined and the crops are gone. The merchants who sold grain and oil have nothing. The vinedressers are out of work along with the farmers. A wailing was heard across the land (1:11). All the trees and gardens and plants are gone and so was the heart of the people. They dried up like the plants, all joy was taken from them (1:12) The locust plague was not just a devastating environmental event, it was a devastation of the soul of the people. Like an open wound, the memories were still fresh and they hurt.

This invasion was from the hand of God and the only relief that could come would be from that same hand. Repentance is what God wanted from His people.

Joel calls the people to repent (1:13, 14).

¹³ Gird yourselves *with sackcloth*
And lament, O priests;
Wail, O ministers of the altar!
Come, spend the night in sackcloth
O ministers of my God,
For the grain offering and the drink offering
Are withheld from the house of your God.
¹⁴ Consecrate a fast,
Proclaim a solemn assembly;
Gather the elders
And all the inhabitants of the land
To the house of the LORD YOUR GOD,
And cry out to the LORD.

It is clear in the book of Joel that God that sent the locust plague (1:15, 2:25). The locust plague was sent because of the sin in the land. *"Gird yourselves with sackcloth and lament, O priests."*

> **"Sackcloth is a coarse, black cloth made from goat's hair that was worn together with the burnt ashes of wood as a sign of mourning for personal and national disaster, as a sign of repentance and at times of prayer for deliverance."** (Bible Gateway dictionary)

Judah's locust plague was a judgment against the sin of the people. The warning begins with the spiritual leaders of the land, the priests. The priests were the ones appointed by God to show the people the way to seek God. They ministered in the Temple at the great altar of sacrifice in the courtyard where sinners brought their sacrificial animals to offer to God. The priests were the mediators between man and God. Ultimately, they were a shadow of the final Lamb of God who would take away the sin of the world. They also were a shadow, or picture, of our Great High Priest, the Lord Jesus Christ (Hebrews 10:1). Priests were God's designated connection between man and God. When they failed in their divinely appointed duties, the way of salvation by faith in the Old Testament was hidden from the people. The corruption and disobedience of the priests caused great spiritual darkness to spread across the land, like a locust plague spread across the land.

God sent the locust plague to get the attention of the people and the priests so they could see that God was serious.

> **"Wail, O ministers of the altar!**
> **Come, spend the night in sackcloth**
> **O ministers of my God,**
> **For the grain offering and the drink offering**
> **Are withheld from the house of your God."** (1:13)

The priests, who were the spiritual leaders of the nation, had failed in their solemn duties and the people were like wandering sheep without a shepherd. What were they supposed to do to get back into God's favor? He tells them the specific steps in the next verse.

> **"Consecrate a fast,**
> **Proclaim a solemn assembly;**
> **Gather the elders**
> **And all the inhabitants of the land**
> **To the house of the Lord your God,**
> **And cry out to the Lord."** (1:14)

SEEKING GOD ACCORDING TO VERSE 14.

1. They needed to set aside time for a special national fast. This was not a small thing like skipping a meal. This fast was a solemn gathering, a time of mourning for sins.
2. All the leaders of the nation were to be spiritual leaders again, being the first to fast and seek God.
3. The entire nation was to join in the time of mourning for their neglect of God.
4. They were to come to the Temple, the place where the priests had departed from God by stopping the offerings (1:13).
5. The leaders were to lead the people in prayer as a nation, crying out to God for mercy.

Because of the locust devastation, they had no grain or meal for the Grain Offerings that God had instructed in the Law (Leviticus two), but they had to begin somewhere to get back on track. The beginning point is always repentance for sin.

Joel then uses the drought to teach the people that God's day is coming. The locust plague they experienced was just the day of the locust. The Day of the Lord is a much more significant event. The Day of the Lord is the day when the Lord has His day.

All eyes are on Him. He is the sovereign King and what He decrees is what happens. This will have a local impact on Judah in the days to come when a different type of locust invasion comes on their land and it will have a future global fulfillment at the second coming of Christ.

But first, back to the drought. The description of the effects of the day of the locust will give hints about the Day of the Lord.

Starvation and drought because of national sin (1:15-20).

15 Alas for the day!
For the day of the LORD is near,
And it will come as destruction from the Almighty.
16 Has not food been cut off before our eyes,
Gladness and joy from the house of our God?
17 The seeds shrivel under their clods;
The storehouses are desolate,
The barns are torn down,
For the grain is dried up.
18 How the beasts groan!
The herds of cattle wander aimlessly
Because there is no pasture for them;
Even the flocks of sheep suffer.
19 To You, O LORD, I cry;
For fire has devoured the pastures of the wilderness
And the flame has burned up all the trees of the field.
20 Even the beasts of the field pant for You;
For the water brooks are dried up
And fire has devoured the pastures of the wilderness.

Joel begins his description by saying that as bad as the locust plague was, what was coming next would be an even greater event being orchestrated by God.

> **"Alas for the day!**
> **For the day of the Lord is near,**
> **And it will come as destruction from the Almighty.**
> **Has not food been cut off before our eyes,**
> **Gladness and joy from the house of our God?"** (1:15, 16)

The priests failed and the people lost their way back to God. There was no joy in the Temple because the sacrifices stopped. The people were hopelessly drifting away from God like a ship that has lost its anchor smashing onto the rocks. Their spiritual lives were cut off but at the same time, their food supply was cut off by the locusts. They were physically and spiritually hurting. To make matters worse, Joel announced new destruction on the land called "the day of the Lord."

The destruction is certain and it comes from "*Shaddai,*" (The Hebrew lexicon "most powerful Shaddai, the Almighty of God). The first time this Hebrew word is used in the Bible was to Abraham.

> **"Now when Abram was ninety-nine years old, the**
> **LORD appeared to Abram and said to him, "I am God**
> **Amighty; Walk before Me, and be blameless."**
> (Genesis 17:1)

The land of Judah had fallen into the snares of false gods, pieces of stone and wood that were powerless to help or save. Now, the Almighty Himself was speaking to the people. They had not heard His name or voice for a long time. His day was coming. The destruction they had faced during the day of the locust was but a glimpse of the day of the Lord that was yet to happen. The description He gives of the locust devastation is a preview of the next chapter when the greater storm is revealed.

"Has not food been cut off before our eyes,
Gladness and joy from the house of our God?
The seeds shrivel under their clods;
The storehouses are desolate,
The barns are torn down,
For the grain is dried up.
How the beasts groan!
The herds of cattle wander aimlessly
Because there is no pasture for them;
Even the flocks of sheep suffer.
To You, O Lord, I cry;
For fire has devoured the pastures of the wilderness
And the flame has burned up all the trees of the field.
Even the beasts of the field pant for You;
For the water brooks are dried up
And fire has devoured the pastures of the wilderness."
(1:16-20)

The locust swarm had caused great hardships on Judah:

- The food chain was destroyed. (1:16)
- The joy of living was gone; even the simplest pleasures like eating were not to be found. (1:16)
- Seeds in gardens and fields stop germinating; there was no water. (1:17)
- The reserves that had been stored were used up, the cupboards were bare. (1:17)
- The barns were no longer in use; they decayed and were torn down. (1:17)
- Everything was bone dry. (1:17)
- The pastures for the cattle were no more and the sounds of starving animals no longer heard across the land. (1:18)
- Cattle and sheep wandered looking for food. (1:18)
- The people weep and cry to God for help. (1:19)
- The dryness has brought on great prairie fires that have swept over the land. (1:19)

- The fires have consumed all the trees. (1:19)
- Man and beast roam about looking for a source of water. (1:20)

The most difficult thing they have been told by the prophet Joel is that the worse is still up ahead. The day of the locust and the great drought is but the beginning of sorrows. If someone had told them to "Cheer up, things could be worse," it would have done no good because things were going to get worse.

The fire that ravaged the land is like a campfire when compared to the fire of the wrath of Shaddai, the Almighty God, who has been angered by the idolatry, corruptions, and oppressions of the people to whom He had given so much.

The larger locust invasion was coming and it is not insects.

Joel Two
THE DAY OF THE LORD IN THE TIME OF JOEL

The day of the locust described in chapter one, as devastating as it was, was only a foretaste of what was coming. These final two chapters introduce the Day of the Lord. Judah had its day, now it's God's day.

The Day of the Lord is a major theme of many of the prophets. It can be used to describe many things:

USAGES OF "THE DAY OF THE LORD" IN THE BIBLE.

- It can be a day when God brings judgment on sin.
- It can refer to the day when God makes Israel the head of the nations.
- It can refer to the time in the future when God will fight for Israel against all their enemies.
- It can refer to the end of the world.
- It can refer to God using Assyria and Babylon to bring His judgment on His people for their sins.
- It can mean the second coming of Jesus.
- It refers to the time of the tribulation when the great day of God's wrath will come.
- It can refer to the final time of the great judgment when the heavens and earth pass away and God sits on His throne to judge the world.
- The fall of Jerusalem was referred to as the Day of the Lord.
- It can refer to any time of great destruction when God's patience runs out and He sends His judgment on the earth.

The general use of the word is a time or season when God takes over and brings about His holy purposes on the earth. It is His day, not man's day.

WHAT DID JOEL MEAN BY THE "DAY OF THE LORD"?

There seem to be four usages in the book of Joel.

- The first is the day of the locusts in chapter one. This was a divine intervention by God to bring judgment on the sins of Judah. It was the day of the Lord.
- The second is found in the chapter we will look at now. God would be sending the Babylonian army to destroy Jerusalem and the Temple and take the people captive.
- The third and fourth usage will be a prophecy at the end of chapter two and in chapter three. It had a partial fulfillment in the first century when Peter quoted the Joel passage but the second half of Joel's prophecy will not be completed until the Tribulation and the Great Day of the Lord comes when Jesus the Messiah returns.

With that background, we will begin chapter two.

A human locust storm is coming (2:1, 2).

¹ Blow a trumpet in Zion,
And sound an alarm on My holy mountain!
Let all the inhabitants of the land tremble,
For the day of the LORD IS COMING;
Surely it is near,
² A day of darkness and gloom,
A day of clouds and thick darkness.
As the dawn is spread over the mountains,

So there is a great and mighty people;
There has never been *anything* like it,
Nor will there be again after it
To the years of many generations.

As noted in the introduction, some commentators believe Joel prophesied during the 8th century B.C. and therefore the invading army described in Joel chapter two is the Assyrian Empire. The book itself is impossible to date accurately so the definitive date is uncertain. Having said that, this author believes the large number of prophets Joel quotes or seems very familiar with were all prophesying at the time of the Babylonian invasion. That places him in the time of the Babylonian captivity in the 6th century B.C. One more thing. The Assyrian invasion was only against Israel, the Northern Kingdom. The Assyrians were stopped by God before they could harm Judah. Joel began chapter two by describing the invasion in Judah which took place during the Babylonian period (2:1).

The *"Day of the Lord"* in this chapter is referring to God using the Babylonian armies to bring His judgment on His people for their sins. The day of the locust in chapter one was a real locust swarm that ruined the Judaean landscape. The invasion of the Babylonian army is poetically phrased to resemble an actual locust swarm. The Babylonians are prophesied to swarm down on Judah and consume the land. This military "locust invasion" will prove to be more devastating than actual locusts.

> **"Blow a trumpet in Zion,**
> **And sound an alarm on My holy mountain!**
> **Let all the inhabitants of the land tremble,**
> **For the day of the Lord is coming;"** (2:1)

The people were accustomed to hearing the blowing of the shofar, the ram's horn used by the priests to call the people to worship. Ihis is different. It was used to blast a warning, a signal of a terror that was coming.

> "The preaching of the prophet increases in its intensity. Behind the locusts, exemplified by them, there is a still more terrible visitation. He sees on the horizon a mustering of a nation hostile to his people, bent on destroying them. Let the priests stir up the people for a fast, and for the defense of their land by the trumpet. The locusts have done their symbolical work, they have left their mark on the country. Now the day of Jehovah, the manifestation of His power, is approaching—it is imminent." (Ellicott's Commentary for English readers)

> "Joel's cry to "blow the trumpet in Zion, sound the alarm on my holy mountain" is the announcement that the day of the Lord "is coming, it is near" (2:1). And like Amos, Joel was announcing that the Lord's coming was not the good news the people had expected, but bad news. The people of Israel looked forward to the day of the Lord as a child today looks forward to Christmas. They thought it would be the day when the Lord would act within history to deliver Israel from her enemies, the day when the Lord would defeat Israel's foes. Not so fast, announces Joel! It is "a day of darkness and gloom" (2:2).
> (Working Preacher commentary)

Just as locust swarms were so large they darkened the sun, so this invasion would result in a time of darkness and gloom.

> "Surely it is near,
> A day of darkness and gloom,
> A day of clouds and thick darkness.
> As the dawn is spread over the mountains,
> So there is a great and mighty people;
> There has never been anything like it,
> Nor will there be again after it
> To the years of many generations." (2:2)

Image: Courtesy of The Bible Project

The military description of these verses and the invasion
identified as a *"great and mighty people"* make it clear that this
is a major military conquest. It will be unlike any Judah has
faced before. God used Assyria to destroy the Northern
Kingdom of Israel before but Assyria was prevented by God to
harm Judah in the south (2 Chronicles 32). That protection was
lifted with the Babylonian invasion. They brought the nation of
Judah to its knees trembling (2:1). History tells us the
Babylonians were fierce.

> **"Therefore He (God) brought up against them the king of
> the Chaldeans who slew their young men with the sword
> in the house of their sanctuary, and had no compassion
> on young man or virgin, old man or infirm; He gave them
> all into his hand. All the articles of the house of God, great
> and small, and the treasures of the house of the Lord, and
> the treasures of the king and of his officers, he brought
> them all to Babylon. Then they burned the house of God
> and broke down the wall of Jerusalem, and burned all its
> fortified buildings with fire and destroyed all its valuable
> articles. Those who had escaped from the sword he**

carried away to Babylon; and they were servants to him
and to his sons until the rule of the kingdom of Persia."
(2 Chronicles 36:17-20)

For Judah, it would be a day of "*darkness and gloom, . . . clouds
and thick darkness*" (2:2). It was the worst thing that had
happened to the people of God. It came upon them like the
sunlight floods the land at sunrise (2:2). It was like a dense
swarm of locusts sweeping over the land, covering the sun.

The human locust storm is described (2:3-11).

³ A fire consumes before them
And behind them a flame burns.
The land is like the garden of Eden before them
But a desolate wilderness behind them,
And nothing at all escapes them.
⁴ Their appearance is like the appearance of horses;
And like war horses, so they run.
⁵ With a noise as of chariots
They leap on the tops of the mountains,
Like the crackling of a flame of fire consuming the stubble,
Like a mighty people arranged for battle.
⁶ Before them the people are in anguish;
All faces turn pale.
⁷ They run like mighty men,
They climb the wall like soldiers;
And they each march in line,
Nor do they deviate from their paths.
⁸ They do not crowd each other,
They march everyone in his path;
When they burst through the defenses,
They do not break ranks.

⁹ They rush on the city,
They run on the wall;
They climb into the houses,
They enter through the windows like a thief.
¹⁰ Before them the earth quakes,
The heavens tremble,
The sun and the moon grow dark
And the stars lose their brightness.
¹¹ The LORD utters His voice before His army;
Surely His camp is very great,
For strong is he who carries out His word.
The day of the LORD is indeed great and very awesome,
And who can endure it?

This author has seen large forest fires. They strike fear in the region. A beautiful mountain of green trees stands quietly before the fire arrives but only burned-out stumps on blackened hillsides remain after the fire passes through. No human effort can stop them, everything in the fire's path is destroyed. Joel described the Babylonian army in the language of a locust invasion and also like the devastation of a great fire. Both strip the land of all living things. This gives some hints about the size of the Babylonian army.

> **"A fire consumes before them**
> **And behind them a flame burns.**
> **The land is like the garden of Eden before them**
> **But a desolate wilderness behind them,**
> **And nothing at all escapes them."** (2:3)

The army is pictured as being very fierce and terrifying. They move with the swiftness of horses. The sound of the advancing army is like the rumbling of chariot wheels (2:4, 5). No mountain or obstacle can stop them, just like a great fire consuming everything in their path (2:5). Everyone who sees them coming shrinks in fear. The people they invade feel weak and hopeless when they see them (2:6).

> "Their appearance is like the appearance of horses;
> And like war horses, so they run.
> With a noise as of chariots
> They leap on the tops of the mountains,
> Like the crackling of a flame of fire consuming the stubble,
> Like a mighty people arranged for battle.
> Before them the people are in anguish;
> All faces turn pale." (2:4-6)

Verses 7-9 gives us a picture of the discipline of the army. We see a large military assembly with a clear objective and each soldier following his assigned place and working in clockwork precision. We are told they march together in a line, never departing from their formation (2:7). Each soldier stays in his place as they march. Even when they attack, they stay in their assigned places in the formation (2:8). Together, as a unit, they rush, run, climb, and seize their enemy. They are a well-trained and disciplined force (2:9).

> "They run like mighty men,
> They climb the wall like soldiers;
> And they each march in line,
> Nor do they deviate from their paths.
> They do not crowd each other,
> They march everyone in his path;
> When they burst through the defenses,
> They do not break ranks.
> They rush on the city,
> They run on the wall;
> They climb into the houses,
> They enter through the windows like a thief." (2:7-9)

There was no army in the world on that day like the Babylonians. Joel, in his poetic way, tells us how they were feared by everyone:

"Before them the earth quakes,
The heavens tremble,
The sun and the moon grow dark
And the stars lose their brightness." (2:10)

But there was something else about the army that intensified the fear of the people of Judah. It wasn't just that the Babylonians were fierce and unstoppable, it was that God had made it clear that He was sending them. The prophet Habakkuk had also warned them:

"I am raising up the Babylonians,
    that ruthless and impetuous people,
who sweep across the whole earth
    to seize dwellings not their own." (Habakkuk 1:6)

Joel also refers to the Babylonian army as God's army in verse 11. The people of Judah would not just be fighting against a foreign invader, they will be fighting their God!

"The Lord utters His voice before His army;
Surely His camp is very great,
For strong is he who carries out His word.
The day of the Lord is indeed great and very awesome,
And who can endure it?" (2:11)

An ancient Mesopotamian tablet showing their marching army in formation. It was found in ancient Ur.

A call again for the people to repent (2:12-17).

¹² "Yet even now," declares the LORD,
"Return to Me with all your heart,
And with fasting, weeping and mourning;
¹³ And rend your heart and not your garments."
Now return to the LORD YOUR GOD,
For He is gracious and compassionate,
Slow to anger, abounding in lovingkindness
And relenting of evil.
¹⁴ Who knows whether He will *not* turn and relent
And leave a blessing behind Him,
Even a grain offering and a drink offering
For the LORD YOUR GOD?
¹⁵ Blow a trumpet in Zion,
Consecrate a fast, proclaim a solemn assembly,
¹⁶ Gather the people, sanctify the congregation,
Assemble the elders,
Gather the children and the nursing infants.
Let the bridegroom come out of his room
And the bride out of her *bridal* chamber.
¹⁷ Let the priests, the LORD'S MINISTERS,
Weep between the porch and the altar,
And let them say, "Spare Your people, O LORD,
And do not make Your inheritance a reproach,
A byword among the nations.
Why should they among the peoples say,
'Where is their God?'"

Amazing words begin the next set of verses. Judah had been warned that great destruction was coming and God would orchestrate it just as He had arranged the locust plague. Locusts, Babylonians, and even God were at war with His rebellious and unfaithful people. Then, like a soft breeze blowing over the mountain that had been blackened with fire, come the next words:

> "'Yet even now,' declares the Lord,
> 'Return to Me with all your heart,
> And with fasting, weeping and mourning;
> And rend your heart and not your garments.'
> Now return to the Lord your God,
> For He is gracious and compassionate,
> Slow to anger, abounding in lovingkindness
> And relenting of evil.
> Who knows whether He will not turn and relent
> And leave a blessing behind Him." (2:12-14)

Yet, even now" He pleads with His people. He was telling the people of Judah, despite everything that is planned against you, won't you please come home to Me. Just come home. You need to come in true repentance, not just with outward signs but with a true heart showing that you are sickened for your sins and disgusted with your idolatry. It has to come from your heart. I don't want you just going through the religious motions (2:12, 13).

Joel tells them If they do that it could prevent a great tragedy. He couldn't guarantee that God would stop the invasion but if they did nothing, judgment would come for certain (2:14).

Joel then told them how to call the nation back to seeking God again (2:15-17).

- Start with a trumpet blast signaling an official national event. The leaders must do this and be convinced it is the right thing to do. (2:15)
- Gather as one people with the elders leading the nation. Each person needed to turn from their sins and set themselves apart to follow God and His Law. (2:16)
- No one is exempt, not even the children and infants. Newlyweds need to come, even delaying their honeymoon.

Nothing is more important than this. (2:16)
- The priests who have failed the people need to be near the great altar of the Temple. They are in tears, for their failure as spiritual leaders. (2:17)
- The priests who repent first should pray for their people that God would spare them from the great calamity that is coming. (2:17)
- If the priests and the people will do this, God will no longer be mocked by the ungodly nations. (2:17)

Joel hated the sins of Judah. He did not want them to abandon God. He did everything he could to help them find their way home. The day Joel looked for was still ahead. The Babylonians did invade and took Judah captive to Babylon for seventy years as God warned. As we noted, the Day of the Lord refers not just to an immediate national judgment for sin, but also looks ahead to a greater day. In this case, Joel describes something not yet seen in the history of the chosen people of God. They have had ups and downs throughout their history, but never have they had a permanent restoration of their land and their God as their King. From 2:18 through the end of the book, **we see a shift to a future time when God will fully heal the land and restore the fortunes of the people, and the sons of Zion will be glad in their God**.

When Judah repents, God will restore His blessing and protection (2:18-20).

[18] Then the LORD WILL BE ZEALOUS FOR HIS LAND
And will have pity on His people.
[19] The LORD WILL ANSWER AND SAY TO HIS PEOPLE,
"Behold, I am going to send you grain, new wine and oil,

And you will be satisfied *in full* with them;
And I will never again make you a reproach among
the nations.
[20] "But I will remove the northern *army* far from you,
And I will drive it into a parched and desolate land,
And its vanguard into the eastern sea,
And its rear guard into the western sea.
And its stench will arise and its foul smell will come up,
For it has done great things."

Important notes:

A DIFFICULT CHALLENGE UNDERSTANDING PROPHETIC PASSAGES.

This new hope section begins with the word, "*then*." This is not saying "if." The day of the repentance and restoration of Judah is going to happen. But when? The descriptions in the last part of Joel takes us to a time when the Messiah will reign over His people in the land of Judah. It speaks of a day when the nations will honor the restored land of Israel. This time could only be the Millennial Reign of Christ.

Verses 18-20 reveal that God has always been jealous for His land and His people. Because of that, He will pity them and bring back abundant crops. His people will be satisfied completely and they will never again be "*a reproach among the nations*" (2:19). The enemies of Israel will be removed far from them; God will drive them out (2:20). God will judge the enemy nations and the slaughter will become a strong stench (2:20).

One of the difficult challenges in understanding prophecies dealing with the end days, especially in a book like Joel, is that it is often difficult to know when the prophet shifts from a current event to an end time description. The introduction to the book of Joel dealt with the dating and interpretation issues associated with Joel.

EXAMPLE FROM JOEL TWO OF THE DIFFICULTY OF INTERPRETATION.

After warning about the coming military invasion in the first part of this chapter, God then calls upon the people of Judah to repent in verse 12. All this was given to Judah in Joel's time.

In verse 27 God promises *"Thus you will know that I am in the midst of Israel, And that I am the Lord your God, and there is no other, and My people will never be put to shame."* This is an end-time event when God lives with his people. This event is still in the future today.

But in the very next verse (2:28), Joel describes a different time when *"It will come about after this that I will pour out My Spirit on all mankind, and your sons and daughters will prophesy, Your old men will dream dreams,"* Peter quoted this passage in Acts 2 and said it was fulfilled on the day of Pentecost in the first century.

> "These people are not drunk, as you suppose. It's only nine in the morning! No, this is what was spoken by the prophet Joel:
> 'In the last days, God says,
> I will pour out my Spirit on all people.
> Your sons and daughters will prophesy,
> your young men will see visions,
> your old men will dream dreams.
> Even on my servants, both men and women,
> I will pour out my Spirit in those days,'" (Acts 2:15-18)

But again, in the second half of Joel's prophecy, quoted by Peter, it describes a different time, the Great Day of the Lord, when the Great Tribulation will take place. This did not happen during the time of Pentecost. Look at the rest of Joel's prophecy quoted by Peter at Pentecost:

> "and they will prophesy.
> I will show wonders in the heavens above

and signs on the earth below,
  blood and fire and billows of smoke.
The sun will be turned to darkness
  and the moon to blood
  before the coming of the great and glorious day
of the Lord.
And everyone who calls
  on the name of the Lord will be saved." (Acts 2:18b-21)

Joel seems to seamlessly move from his time to the first century to the Tribulation period to the Millennial Reign of Christ almost in a fluid fashion. Whenever you read various commentaries on Joel you will find they often struggle to fit the pieces together. It is hard to make an outline when one passage as we have seen can go from the day of Pentecost to the end of the world and back in one passage, even back-to-back verses.

Don't let this be a discouragement. We do understand more and more as we spend time in God's Word. There still remains some mysteries, the greatest of them all is God Himself. But the fact that we can't understand everything about God only makes us learn all the more, something we will do for all eternity.

Judah will be restored on that great day (2:21-27).

²¹ Do not fear, O land, rejoice and be glad,
For the LORD has done great things.
²² Do not fear, beasts of the field,
For the pastures of the wilderness have turned green,
For the tree has borne its fruit,
The fig tree and the vine have yielded in full.
²³ So rejoice, O sons of Zion,
And be glad in the LORD your God;
For He has given you the early rain for *your* vindication.

And He has poured down for you the rain,
The early and latter rain as before.
24 The threshing floors will be full of grain,
And the vats will overflow with the new wine and oil.
25 "Then I will make up to you for the years
That the swarming locust has eaten,
The creeping locust, the stripping locust and the gnawing locust,
My great army which I sent among you.
26 "You will have plenty to eat and be satisfied
And praise the name of the LORD your God,
Who has dealt wondrously with you;
Then My people will never be put to shame.
27 "Thus you will know that I am in the midst of Israel,
And that I am the LORD your God,
And there is no other;
And My people will never be put to shame.

For all believers, the thoughts of a new heaven, new earth, and resurrected bodies with no more curse, make our hearts beat stronger and bring hope to our hearts. For the people of Judah, who had gone through difficult droughts and pestilence, Joel's words gave them the same hope. No matter how bad it had been, or would be, there is light at the end of the journey for the faithful, the remnant of Israel.

A day is coming when Judah will no longer fear the invading nations. They will not fear wild beasts or having droughts again (2:21, 22). The fig tree and grapevines will flourish again. God will bring the early Autumn and the latter Spring rains, blessings will flow (2:23). The grain will again fill the fields and wine will overflow the vats (2:24). God will restore all that the locusts have eaten (2:25).

"It will strike you at once that the locusts did not eat the years: the locusts ate the fruits of the years' labor, the harvests of the fields; so that the meaning of the restoration of the years must be the restoration of those fruits and of those harvests which the locusts consumed. You cannot have back your time; but there is a strange and wonderful way in which God can give back to you the wasted blessings, the unripened fruits of years over which you mourned. The fruits of wasted years may yet be yours." (Spurgeon)

Pestilence will be only a memory and all losses made up multi-fold (2:25). Hunger will become ancient history, never to afflict anyone again. No shame will ever be felt again by a child of God (2:26). This can only be describing a future day when God will remove all pain and bless his faithful believers.

But the best part of all. God will live among His people (2:27). When will that happen. Revelation gives us a glimpse:

"Then I saw a new heaven and a new earth, for the first heaven and the first earth had passed away, and there was no longer any sea. I saw the Holy City, the new Jerusalem, coming down out of heaven from God, prepared as a bride beautifully dressed for her husband. And I heard a loud voice from the throne saying, 'Look! God's dwelling place is now among the people, and he will dwell with them. They will be his people, and God himself will be with them and be their God. 'He will wipe every tear from their eyes. There will be no more death' or mourning or crying or pain, for the old order of things has passed away.'" (Revelation 21:1-4)

In the next section we come to one of the prophecies that has a dual fulfillment. It is quoted in the New Testament by the Apostle Peter (Acts 2). As the others, it has complex components making it difficult to fully understand.

The future Great Day of the Lord (2:28-32).

28 "It will come about after this
That I will pour out My Spirit on all mankind;
And your sons and daughters will prophesy,
Your old men will dream dreams,
Your young men will see visions.
29 "Even on the male and female servants
I will pour out My Spirit in those days.
30 "I will display wonders in the sky and on the earth,
Blood, fire and columns of smoke.
31 "The sun will be turned into darkness
And the moon into blood
Before the great and awesome day of the LORD comes.
32 "And it will come about that whoever calls on the name of the LORD
Will be delivered;
For on Mount Zion and in Jerusalem
There will be those who escape,
As the LORD has said,
Even among the survivors whom the LORD calls.

This passage was quoted by Peter to the crowds on the day of Pentecost in Acts 2. It is viewed in several ways. These are the major positions:

1. Peter was not saying the prophecy of Joel was fulfilled in the Pentecost moment. He was saying that it is still a future prophecy about the end times. The people were seeing what would happen in the end times when the Spirit of God is poured out. The events then were a foretaste of the future.
2. The prophecy of Joel was partially fulfilled. The first part in 2:28, 29 at Pentecost and the following verses will be fulfilled at a future time.

These are both possibilities. I find one difference between Joel 2:28-32 and Acts 2:17-21. Peter's quotation adds four words that could explain one of the two views better. The four additional words in the Acts passage have been underlined:

> **"Then Peter stood up with the Eleven, raised his voice and addressed the crowd: 'Fellow Jews and all of you who live in Jerusalem, let me explain this to you; listen carefully to what I say. These people are not drunk, as you suppose. It's only nine in the morning! No, this is what was spoken by the prophet Joel:**
>
> **In the last days, God says,**
>
> > **"I will pour out my Spirit on all people.**
> > **Your sons and daughters will prophesy,**
> > **your young men will see visions,**
> > **your old men will dream dreams.**
> > **Even on my servants, both men and women,**
> > **I will pour out my Spirit in those days,**
> > <u>**and they will prophesy.**</u>
> >
> > > **I will show wonders in the heavens above**
> > > **and signs on the earth below,**
> > > **blood and fire and billows of smoke.**
> > > **The sun will be turned to darkness**
> > > **and the moon to blood**
> > > **before the coming of the great and glorious day of the Lord.**
> > > **And everyone who calls**
> > > **on the name of the Lord will be saved.""" (Acts 2:14-21)**

It is clearly stated in Acts 2:16 that verses 17 and 18 were fulfilled when the Holy Spirit manifested Himself on the day of Pentecost and signs and wonders accompanied the birth of the Church. The events that followed did not occur on that day but more closely resemble the last days Jesus said were coming just before He returns. Read what Jesus said:

> **"There will be signs in sun and moon and stars, and on the earth dismay among nations, in perplexity at the roaring of the sea and the waves, men fainting from fear and the expectation of the things which are coming upon the world; for the powers of the heavens will be shaken. Then they will see the Son of Man coming in a cloud with power and great glory."** (Luke 21:25-27)

Those four words, "***and they will prophesy,***" come at the exact break of Joel's prophecy between what is happening in Peter's time and what will happen at the end of the Great Tribulation just before Christ returns. If the dual prophecy method of interpretation is correct, then what those four words are saying is that there would be people filled with the Holy Spirit at the time of Pentecost who will repeat the second half of Joel's full prophecy and tell that it would come at a future time. That was not understood until the first century.

Whichever way we see it, there is no doubt that part of Joel's prophecy to his people was a future event or a two-part event. There was coming a day when the Holy Spirit would have a strong influence on the affairs of men and His ministry would increase as the days grow closer to the end. At the very end, before Christ returns, great wonders in the sky will be seen by those living in that time. Then the Great Tribulation Jesus talked about will come on the earth. It is the Great Day of the Lord. Anyone who calls on the name of the Lord will be saved. It is the last chance.

Other prophets also spoke of this time. Here are four passages:

> **"The fortress will be abandoned,**
> **the noisy city deserted;**
> **citadel and watchtower will become a wasteland forever,**
> **the delight of donkeys, a pasture for flocks,**
> **till the Spirit is poured on us from on high,**

133

and the desert becomes a fertile field,
and the fertile field seems like a forest.
The Lord's justice will dwell in the desert,
his righteousness live in the fertile field.
The fruit of that righteousness will be peace;
its effect will be quietness and confidence forever."
(Isaiah 32:14-17)

"For I will pour water on the thirsty land,
and streams on the dry ground;
I will pour out my Spirit on your offspring,
and my blessing on your descendants." (Isaiah 44:3)

"'The days are coming,' declares the Lord,
'when I will make a new covenant
with the people of Israel
and with the people of Judah . . .
This is the covenant I will make with the people of Israel
after that time," declares the Lord.
I will put my law in their minds
and write it on their hearts.
I will be their God,'" (Jeremiah 31:31, 33)

"For I will take you out of the nations; I will gather you
from all the countries and bring you back into your own
land. I will sprinkle clean water on you, and you will be
clean; I will cleanse you from all your impurities and from
all your idols. I will give you a new heart and put a new
spirit in you; I will remove from you your heart of stone
and give you a heart of flesh. And I will put my Spirit in
you and move you to follow my decrees and be careful to
keep my laws. Then you will live in the land I gave your
ancestors; you will be my people, and I will be your God."
(Ezekiel 36:24-28)

A great day is coming. A great day of judgment. A great day of
people calling on the name of the Lord. A great day for Israel
and Judah when God gathers His Remnant, the elect from the
four winds. A great day when God will make all things new and

a great day when the New Jerusalem descends from heaven to the new earth. A great day is coming.

But we aren't finished. Joel has one more chapter to go.

Joel Three
THE GREAT DAY OF THE LORD WILL COME.

The third chapter is about the final justice of God. He will right all wrongs against His people. Israel and Judah have paid greatly for their sins. They faced droughts, fires, locusts, enemy army invasions, and captivity at the hands of the wicked nations. Joel describes the day of reckoning that will come upon the wicked nations. He transports us to that end time when Judah will be restored to Mount Zion and God will dwell with them forever.

God will restore Judah and judge those who conspired against His chosen people (3:1-3).

[1] "For behold, in those days and at that time,
When I restore the fortunes of Judah and Jerusalem,
[2] I will gather all the nations
And bring them down to the valley of Jehoshaphat.
Then I will enter into judgment with them there
On behalf of My people and My inheritance, Israel,
Whom they have scattered among the nations;
And they have divided up My land.

³ "They have also cast lots for My people,
Traded a boy for a harlot
And sold a girl for wine that they may drink.

A place is mentioned in verse two that may not be an actual place. The word is "Jehoshaphat." He was the king of Judah, the son of King Asa. He reigned 25 years and is described as one of the best, most dedicated to God, and prosperous kings of Judah. The valley that would be associated with him would be the Kidron valley in Jerusalem between the city and the mount of Olives. The phrase, "valley of Jehoshaphat," is only used twice in the entire Bible and both are in this final chapter of Joel. Here is the other reference:

> "Let the nations be aroused and come up to the
> valley of Jehoshaphat, for there I will sit to judge
> all the surrounding nations." (3:12)

The meaning of the word "*Jehoshaphat*" is "Jehovah has judged." Joel also refers to this valley as the "valley of decision" (3:14). God is saying He will gather "all the nations" in this valley. The two best possibilities are:

1. There is one valley in Scripture where the nations of the world will gather against Israel. That valley is Megiddo where the battle of Armageddon will be fought. It is a large valley in northern Israel. Joel could be referring to that great day when God will defeat all of Israel's enemies. This could be the valley of "Jehovah has judged."

2. It could be referring to the Kidron Valley outside of Jerusalem. When Jesus returns, we know it will be on the Mount of Olives. His foot will touch down there and cause the mountain to split forming a valley in the Kidron region (Zechariah 14:5).

God's judgment against the nations at this time will be for His people as justice against all her tormenters over the centuries:

> **"On behalf of My people and My inheritance, Israel,**
> **Whom they have scattered among the nations."** (3:2)

At this time God will restore the fortunes of Israel that the nations have plundered (3:1). God will restore the years the locusts had eaten (2:25). We learn also that God is angered over a heartless practice of the enemy nations:

> **"They have also cast lots for My people,**
> **Traded a boy for a harlot**
> **And sold a girl for wine that they may drink."** (3:3)

Many captives were taken in every battle. The enemies of Israel would usually take them as slaves. In the Roman era, Titus captured Jerusalem and destroyed Herod's temple. Rome took 50,000 captives and used them for slave labor to build the Roman Colosseum. Every nation used slave labor to build its empire. Life was cheap to the victors and nowhere is it more evident than the practice soldiers and leaders used. They would trade slaves for the favors of prostitutes. They would use them as gambling money or even use them as currency to buy wine to get drunk (3:3). The nations devalued what God valued. It is time for God to repay the nations for this sin.

God will repay Israel's enemies for their mistreatment of His children (3:4-8).

[4] Moreover, what are you to Me, O Tyre, Sidon and all the regions of Philistia? Are you rendering Me a recompense? But if you do recompense Me, swiftly and speedily I will

return your recompense on your head. [5] Since you have taken My silver and My gold, brought My precious treasures to your temples, [6] and sold the sons of Judah and Jerusalem to the Greeks in order to remove them far from their territory, [7] behold, I am going to arouse them from the place where you have sold them, and return your recompense on your head. [8] Also I will sell your sons and your daughters into the hand of the sons of Judah, and they will sell them to the Sabeans, to a distant nation," for the LORD has spoken.

Tyre, Sidon, and the Philistines were guilty in the past of breaking covenants, capturing people from Israel and Judah, and selling them as slaves to Edom (See the Amos chapter one commentary for detailed information). Their treachery was never forgotten by God and His justice was due. They had also stolen prized possessions of the Temple and silver and gold. Retaliation may have been held back for a while but the selling of God's people to the Edomites and Greeks would not go unpunished (3:4-7). They would one day be turned over to the hands of the children of Judah who would, in turn, send them into exile into distant lands, like southern Saudi Arabia (land of the Sabeans). Their wickedness would come back on their heads. They would reap what they had sowed (3:8).

What the nations did not understand was when they hurt the apple of God's eye it was literally like poking God in the eye. Saul persecuted the early Christians and when the risen Christ stopped his reign of terror on the road to Damascus, He said to Saul, *"Saul, Saul, why are you persecuting Me? (Acts 9:4).*

Every pain inflicted against Israel and Judah was pain inflicted against God almighty. He is not One you want to anger. Tyre, Sidon, and the Philistines learned that.

The day of judgment for the nations has arrived (3:9-17).

⁹ Proclaim this among the nations:
Prepare a war; rouse the mighty men!
Let all the soldiers draw near, let them come up!
¹⁰ Beat your plowshares into swords
And your pruning hooks into spears;
Let the weak say, "I am a mighty man."
¹¹ Hasten and come, all you surrounding nations,
And gather yourselves there.
Bring down, O LORD, Your mighty ones.
¹² Let the nations be aroused
And come up to the valley of Jehoshaphat,
For there I will sit to judge
All the surrounding nations.
¹³ Put in the sickle, for the harvest is ripe.
Come, tread, for the wine press is full;
The vats overflow, for their wickedness is great.
¹⁴ Multitudes, multitudes in the valley of decision!
For the day of the LORD is near in the valley of decision.
¹⁵ The sun and moon grow dark
And the stars lose their brightness.
¹⁶ The LORD roars from Zion
And utters His voice from Jerusalem,
And the heavens and the earth tremble.
But the LORD is a refuge for His people
And a stronghold to the sons of Israel.
¹⁷ Then you will know that I am the LORD your God,
Dwelling in Zion, My holy mountain.
So Jerusalem will be holy,
And strangers will pass through it no more.

The day of war will come. This is the final battle, unlike and battle the world has seen. It is the world versus Israel. It is Israel plus God. That final battle is described in other Scriptures:

THE BATTLE OF ARMAGEDDON.

"The sixth angel poured out his bowl on the great river, the Euphrates; and its water was dried up, so that the way would be prepared for the kings from the east.
And I saw coming out of the mouth of the dragon and out of the mouth of the beast and out of the mouth of the false prophet, three unclean spirits like frogs; for they are spirits of demons, performing signs, which go out to the kings of the whole world, to gather them together for the war of the great day of God, the Almighty. ("Behold, I am coming like a thief. Blessed is the one who stays awake and keeps his clothes, so that he will not walk about naked and men will not see his shame.") And they gathered them together to the place which in Hebrew is called Har-Magedon." (Revelation 16:12-16)

JESUS RETURNS TO DEFEAT THE ENEMIES OF ISRAEL.

"And I saw heaven opened, and behold, a white horse, and He who sat on it is called Faithful and True, and in righteousness He judges and wages war. His eyes are a flame of fire, and on His head are many diadems; and He has a name written on Him which no one knows except Himself. He is clothed with a robe dipped in blood, and His name is called The Word of God. And the armies which are in heaven, clothed in fine linen, white and clean, were following Him on white horses. From His mouth comes a sharp sword, so that with it He may strike down the nations, and He will rule them with a rod of iron; and He treads the wine press of the fierce wrath of God, the Almighty. And on His robe and on His thigh He has a name written, "KING OF KINGS, AND LORD OF LORDS."
(Revelation 19:11-16)

JESUS OWN DESCRIPTION OF THOSE DAYS.

"But immediately after the tribulation of those days the sun will be darkened, and the moon will not give its light, and the stars will fall from the sky, and the powers of the heavens will be shaken. And then the sign of the Son of Man will appear in the sky, and then all the tribes of the earth will mourn, and they will see the Son of Man coming on the clouds of the sky with power and great glory. And He will send forth His angels with a great trumpet and they will gather together His elect from the four winds, from one end of the sky to the other." (Matthew 24:29-31)

As you read through our passage, Joel 3:9-17, you will see many of the same features described by John in Revelation and the words of Jesus. Let's look at each one of them:

IT BEGINS WITH A PROCLAMATION OF WAR (3:9).

"Proclaim this among the nations:
Prepare a war; rouse the mighty men!
Let all the soldiers draw near, let them come up!" (3:9)

This is a proclamation against God and His chosen people. The Psalmist described the futility of fighting against the Almighty.

"Why are the nations in an uproar
And the peoples devising a vain thing?
The kings of the earth take their stand
And the rulers take counsel together
Against the Lord and against His Anointed, saying,
'Let us tear their fetters apart
And cast away their cords from us!'
He who sits in the heavens laughs,
The Lord scoffs at them.
Then He will speak to them in His anger
And terrify them in His fury, saying,

'But as for Me, I have installed My King
Upon Zion, My holy mountain.'" (Psalm 2:1-6)

THE WEAPONS OF WAR ARE PREPARED (3:10).

"Beat your plowshares into swords
And your pruning hooks into spears;
Let the weak say, "I am a mighty man." (3:10)

The people will take their farming equipment and turn them into swords. It is interesting that when the war is over and God gets the victory, His people are commanded to gather the swords and turn them back into farming equipment (plowshares). Peace will be established and it will be like the Garden of Eden later and man will no longer have to learn war any more.

"And He will judge between the nations, And will render decisions for many peoples; And they will hammer their swords into plowshares and their spears into pruning hooks. Nation will not lift up sword against nation, and never again will they learn war." (Isaiah 2:4)

THE NATIONS ARE INVITED TO THEIR DESTRUCTION (3:11-13).

"Hasten and come, all you surrounding nations,
And gather yourselves there.
Bring down, O Lord, Your mighty ones.
Let the nations be aroused
And come up to the valley of Jehoshaphat,
For there I will sit to judge
All the surrounding nations.
Put in the sickle, for the harvest is ripe.
Come, tread, for the wine press is full;
The vats overflow, for their wickedness is great."
(3:11-13)

The nations are all invited to come to the Valley of Jehoshaphat, the place of the judgment of Jehovah (3:12). "Come quickly," God says (3:11), and gather together for the great war. The nations will be in for a surprising defeat. It is described in the language of a grape harvest and the crushing of the grapes. God will cut down all the vines with His sickle, the blood will flow so much that when He presses them in the winepress of His wrath the wine vat will overflow. The sin of the nations is great and so is the final slaughter. This is the war to end all wars.

THE VALLEY OF DECISION (3:14).

> **"Multitudes, multitudes in the valley of decision!**
> **For the day of the Lord is near in the valley of decision."**
> (3:14)

Here is how one commentator described this verse:

> **"Multitudes, multitudes in the valley of decision! Joel looked out upon the Valley of Jehoshaphat at the Battle of Armageddon, and sees multitudes facing their eternal fate – truly, it is a valley of decision, and those who fight against the LORD and His Messiah are in the wrong place in the valley of decision, ultimately fulfilled at the Battle of Armageddon."** (David Guzik)

There are many today in our world who are faced with the same decision. Do we follow God or do we take our stand against God? There is no neutral ground. It is a spiritual war and we have to pick the right side. Every person from every nation that chooses to stand against God in that great end-times conflict will know they made a wrong decision. The consequences of this decision are eternal.

THE GREAT DAY OF THE LORD (3:15-17).

"The sun and moon grow dark
And the stars lose their brightness.
The Lord roars from Zion
And utters His voice from Jerusalem,
And the heavens and the earth tremble.
But the Lord is a refuge for His people
And a stronghold to the sons of Israel.
Then you will know that I am the Lord your God,
Dwelling in Zion, My holy mountain.
So Jerusalem will be holy,
And strangers will pass through it no more." (3:15-17)

Many prophets looked ahead to the final day of the Lord when the heavens will shake at the power of His presence, sin will be judged, and His people restored to fellowship and to their land. Listen first to Isaiah:

"Wail, for the day of the Lord is near!
It will come as destruction from the Almighty.
Therefore all hands will fall limp,
And every man's heart will melt.
... Behold, the day of the Lord is coming,
Cruel, with fury and burning anger,
To make the land a desolation;
And He will exterminate its sinners from it.
For the stars of heaven and their constellations
Will not flash forth their light;
The sun will be dark when it rises
And the moon will not shed its light.
Thus I will punish the world for its evil
And the wicked for their iniquity;" (Isaiah 13:6, 7, 9-11)

The prophet Zephaniah has a few things to add:

"Shout for joy, O daughter of Zion!
Shout in triumph, O Israel!
Rejoice and exult with all your heart,

144

O daughter of Jerusalem!
The Lord has taken away His judgments against you,
He has cleared away your enemies.
The King of Israel, the Lord, is in your midst;
You will fear disaster no more.
. . . "The Lord your God is in your midst,
A victorious warrior.
. . . "Behold, I am going to deal at that time
With all your oppressors,
. . . "At that time I will bring you in,
Even at the time when I gather you together;
Indeed, I will give you renown and praise
Among all the peoples of the earth,
When I restore your fortunes before your eyes,
Says the Lord." (Zephaniah 3:14, 15, 17, 19 , 20)

All of Ezekiel chapters 38 and 39 contain descriptions about the Great Day of the Lord. Here is one small part:

"Therefore wait for Me," declares the Lord,
"For the day when I rise up as a witness.
Indeed, My decision is to gather nations,
To assemble kingdoms,
To pour out on them My indignation,
All My burning anger;
For all the earth will be devoured
By the fire of My zeal." (Ezekiel 38:8)

The Great Day of the Lord will be unlike any other time in human history. There will be signs in the heavens and on earth. These will come after a Great Tribulation Jesus told about. Afterward, Jesus will reign on the earth when the day of judgment is complete. His remnant people will be restored in the land God promised.

This is described in the final part of Joel's prophecy.

The Lord will bless Judah on Mount Zion (3:18-21).

¹⁸ And in that day
The mountains will drip with sweet wine,
And the hills will flow with milk,
And all the brooks of Judah will flow with water;
And a spring will go out from the house of the LORD
To water the valley of Shittim.
¹⁹ Egypt will become a waste,
And Edom will become a desolate wilderness,
Because of the violence done to the sons of Judah,
In whose land they have shed innocent blood.
²⁰ But Judah will be inhabited forever
And Jerusalem for all generations.
²¹ And I will avenge their blood which I have not avenged,
For the LORD dwells in Zion.

God's creation, which was cursed when Adam and Eve fell in the garden of Eden, will be restored. It will produce crops in abundance again. It will be as Eden once was with trees and springs and abundant crops filling the hills (3:18).

> "Then the lame will leap like a deer,
> And the tongue of the mute will shout for joy.
> For waters will break forth in the wilderness
> And streams in the Arabah.
> The scorched land will become a pool
> And the thirsty ground springs of water;
> In the haunt of jackals, its resting place,
> Grass becomes reeds and rushes.
> A highway will be there, a roadway,
> And it will be called the Highway of Holiness.
> The unclean will not travel on it,
> But it will be for him who walks that way." (Isaiah 35:6-8)

Ezekiel describes the abundance of the earth when God restores all things. The description of John in Revelation is similar when describing the new earth.

> **"By the river on its bank, on one side and on the other, will grow all kinds of trees for food. Their leaves will not wither and their fruit will not fail. They will bear every month because their water flows from the sanctuary, and their fruit will be for food and their leaves for healing."** (Ezekiel 47:12)

> **"Then he showed me a river of the water of life, clear as crystal, coming from the throne of God and of the Lamb, in the middle of its street. On either side of the river was the tree of life, bearing twelve kinds of fruit, yielding its fruit every month; and the leaves of the tree were for the healing of the nations. There will no longer be any curse; and the throne of God and of the Lamb will be in it, and His bond-servants will serve Him."** (Revelation 22:1-3)

GOD WILL AVENGE THE BLOOD OF HIS CHILDREN BY ENEMY NATIONS (3:19-21).

> **"Egypt will become a waste,**
> **And Edom will become a desolate wilderness,**
> **Because of the violence done to the sons of Judah,**
> **In whose land they have shed innocent blood.**
> **But Judah will be inhabited forever**
> **And Jerusalem for all generations.**
> **And I will avenge their blood which I have not avenged,**
> **For the Lord dwells in Zion."** (3:19-21)

The book of Joel has chronicled the journey of Judah. We began with the day of the locust and then a different type of locust, the Babylonians, who were used by God to discipline His wayward children. Both events were orchestrated by God. Then we went to the day of Pentecost when the Day of the Lord resulted in the birth of the church. Finally we were tansported to the Great Day of the Lord. God will vindicate His people with a great battle and victory . A new world will be established with eternal hope for God's people. All enemies will be forever vanquished.

Speaking of Judah's enemies, here is what the prophet Zechariah wrote:

> **"Now this will be the plague with which the Lord will strike all the peoples who have gone to war against Jerusalem; their flesh will rot while they stand on their feet, and their eyes will rot in their sockets, and their tongue will rot in their mouth. It will come about in that day that a great panic from the Lord will fall on them; and they will seize one another's hand, and the hand of one will be lifted against the hand of another. Judah also will fight at Jerusalem; and the wealth of all the surrounding nations will be gathered, gold and silver and garments in great abundance. So also like this plague will be the plague on the horse, the mule, the camel, the donkey and all the cattle that will be in those camps."**
> (Zechariah 14:12-15)

Then Jerusalem and the land of Judah will be inhabited again forever by the people of God and Joel ends his book with the greatest promise of all:

"For the LORD dwells in Zion." (3:21)

"For the LORD dwells in Zion."
Joel 3:21

NAHUM

Nineveh's final destruction is predicted and described.

"Woe to the bloody city, completely full of lies and pillage;

"Behold, I am against you," declares the LORD OF HOSTS."

Nahum 3:1, 5

Introduction

What do we know about Nahum?

We know almost nothing about the prophet. The first verse tells us he was an Elkoshite. He came from a town called Elkosh. Most scholars identify this as the town in southern Judah where Micah the prophet grew up. In 3:8 Nahum describes the fall of No-Amon (Thebes) on the Nile river and he prophesied about the destruction of Nineveh. These dates put the writing of Nahum around 663 and 654 B.C. which meant he preached during the reign of the evil King Manasseh of Judah, one of the worst times in Judah's history.

> "Manasseh was twelve years old when he became king, and he reigned fifty-five years in Jerusalem. He did evil in the sight of the Lord according to the abominations of the nations whom the Lord dispossessed before the sons of Israel. For he rebuilt the high places which Hezekiah his father had broken down; he also erected altars for the Baals and made Asherim, and worshiped all the host of heaven and served them. He built altars in the house of the Lord of which the Lord had said, 'My name shall be in Jerusalem forever.' For he built altars for all the host of heaven in the two courts of the house of the Lord. He made his sons pass through the fire in the valley of Ben-hinnom; and he practiced witchcraft, used divination, practiced sorcery and dealt with mediums and spiritists. He did much evil in the sight of the Lord, provoking Him to anger."
> (2 Chronicles 33:1-6)

Nahum's name means "Comforter." His calling was to preach against the "great city" of Nineveh. About 100 years before Nahum, Jonah had been sent by God to warn Nineveh of approaching judgment and the city repented giving it a reprieve for a time (760 B.C.). The city had fallen again into depravity and angered God. It was time to declare its final destruction and God chose Nahum to announce God's justice against Nineveh.

The book of Nahum.

Nahum is a unique book. It does not focus its message on the sins of God's people but keeps the spotlight on the nature of God and the evil of Nineveh and its upcoming destruction. Nahum had much to abhor in the land of Judah with King Manasseh in command, but his task was to finish the story of Nineveh. They had been given a great opportunity to reform after they turned from their evil in Jonah's time. When any people know the way of righteousness and choose to embrace sin, the day of grace will end and the day of wrath will come. That day had come. Nahum, the "comforter," would be a comfort to Judah knowing that their tormenter, Assyria, was going to be judged.

The book is written in a Hebrew poetry style common to many of the prophets. Parallelisms are used throughout. Lines are repeated with different descriptions, building on the previous line or lines. Here is a sample of that poetry style. Nahum even uses the poetry style to sound like the drama of a battle scene:

> **"Woe to the bloody city, completely full of lies and pillage;**
> **Her prey never departs.**
> **The noise of the whip,**
> **The noise of the rattling of the wheel,**
> **Galloping horses**
> **And bounding chariots!**
> **Horsemen charging,**
> **Swords flashing, spears gleaming,**
> **Many slain, a mass of corpses,**
> **And countless dead bodies—**
> **They stumble over the dead bodies!"** (3:1-3)

Another interesting feature of Nahum's writing is the use of Hebrew acrostic style. Psalm 119 is an example of this where each set of poems begins with a different letter of the Hebrew alphabet. It would be like an English language poem starting the first line with "A", the second line with "B", the third with "C", and so on. Nahum did not write the entire book like that but a large portion in that style.

Chapter one is a song to God, a psalm of Nahum, to the greatness and justice of God. The second chapter is about God's condemnation of Nineveh and its coming destruction. The third section is what some people refer to as a taunt, a mockery of the Assyrian nation. It is a celebration of Assyria's downfall. This is an example:

> **"Your shepherds are sleeping, O king of Assyria;**
> **Your nobles are lying down.**
> **Your people are scattered on the mountains**
> **And there is no one to regather them.**
> **There is no relief for your breakdown,**

Your wound is incurable.
All who hear about you
Will clap their hands over you,
For on whom has not your evil passed continually?"
(3:18, 19)

Nahum simple outline.

I. The awesomeness of God.

II. The coming destruction of Nineveh.

III. Nahum mocks and celebrates the fall of Assyria.

Note: The ruins of Nineveh today are in Mosul, Iraq.

Nahum One

God is awesome (1:1-8).

¹ The oracle of Nineveh. The book of the vision of Nahum the Elkoshite.

² A jealous and avenging God is the LORD;
The LORD is avenging and wrathful.
The LORD takes vengeance on His adversaries,
And He reserves wrath for His enemies.
³ The LORD is slow to anger and great in power,
And the LORD will by no means leave *the guilty* unpunished.
In whirlwind and storm is His way,
And clouds are the dust beneath His feet.
⁴ He rebukes the sea and makes it dry;
He dries up all the rivers.

Bashan and Carmel wither;
The blossoms of Lebanon wither.
⁵ Mountains quake because of Him
And the hills dissolve;
Indeed the earth is upheaved by His presence,
The world and all the inhabitants in it.
⁶ Who can stand before His indignation?
Who can endure the burning of His anger?
His wrath is poured out like fire
And the rocks are broken up by Him.
⁷ The LORD is good,
A stronghold in the day of trouble,
And He knows those who take refuge in Him.
⁸ But with an overflowing flood
He will make a complete end of its site,
And will pursue His enemies into darkness.

THE BURDEN OF NINEVEH (1:1).

In verse one, the Hebrew word *Massa* translated "oracle" is often rendered "burden." Verse one describes Nineveh as a burden. It was a burden to the people of Judah and Nahum. We think of a burden as a heavy weight or load to carry. Nineveh, the capital of Assyria, had been a torment to Judah for a long time. They were the bully of the world, enslaving nations, and conquering everyone in their path. They brought unimaginable grief to all the regions. His oracle or utterance of doom on Nineveh was a comforting word to the people of Judah. Nahum lived up to the meaning of his name, "comforter."

GOD DISPLAYS HIS WRATH ON HIS ENEMIES (1:2-3).

"A jealous and avenging God is the Lord;
The Lord is avenging and wrathful.
The Lord takes vengeance on His adversaries,

And He reserves wrath for His enemies.
The Lord is slow to anger and great in power,
And the Lord will by no means leave the
guilty unpunished.
In whirlwind and storm is His way,
And clouds are the dust beneath His feet." (1:2-3)

Jealousy is not a positive attribute. We tend to see a word like that and think of it as being selfish and small. Shakespeare called it "the green-eyed monster." It is also destructive when describing a man or a woman. It produces hostility towards others who have things we don't. It is a sin because it is coveting, which God warned against. How then can God be called Jealous (1:2)?

> "You shall not make for yourself an idol, or any likeness of what is in heaven above or on the earth beneath or in the water under the earth. You shall not worship them or serve them; for I, the LORD your God, am a jealous God." (Exodus 20:4-5)

THE MEANING OF GOD'S JEALOUSY.

> "The root idea in the Old Testament word *jealous* is to become intensely red. It seems to refer to the changing color of the face, the rising heat of the emotions which are associated with intense zeal or fervor over something dear to us. Both the Old and New Testament words for jealousy are also translated 'zeal.' Being jealous and being zealous are essentially the same thing in the Bible. God is zealous—eager about protecting what is precious to Him." (Bible .org)

> "God is not jealous *of* us: He is jealous *for* us." (Redpath in Law and Liberty)

What is precious to God? His people are precious to Him and He protects His children. Most importantly, His holy name and reputation are precious and He rightfully protects that. This is why He hates anything that replaces Him, like idols. God is jealous for His holy name. He abhors any use of His name vainly or thoughtlessly.

> **"I am the LORD, that is My name;**
> **I will not give My glory to another,**
> **Nor My praise to graven images."** (Isaiah 42:8)

Nineveh had struck the apple of God's eye when they destroyed Israel. Assyria threatened Judah and the Lord would protect His sheep from the wolves. All harm done to His own would be avenged. The justice of God flows from His holy character.

> **"The Lord is avenging and wrathful.**
> **The Lord takes vengeance on His adversaries,**
> **And He reserves wrath for His enemies."** (1:2)

The jealousy of God is bad news for His enemies, but good news for His children. The apostle Paul put it this way, *"If God is for us, who is against us?"* (Romans 8:31). God's great power can lift His children out of any danger and crush His enemies into dust.

> **"The Lord is slow to anger and great in power,**
> **And the Lord will by no means leave the guilty unpunished.**
> **In whirlwind and storm is His way,**
> **And clouds are the dust beneath His feet."** (1:3)

"Who is like the Lord our God, who is enthroned on high?" asked the Psalmist (Psalm 113:5). He will not allow anyone to drag His holy name into the mud without punishment. He may show restraint for a while, being slow to anger, but the offender must face the *"whirlwind and storm"* of His wrath against sin.

> **"For the wrath of God is revealed from heaven against all ungodliness and unrighteousness of men who suppress the truth in unrighteousness."** (Romans 1:18)

And this was the oracle, or burden of Nahum. The cup of iniquity of the Ninevites was not just full, it was overflowing. The whirlwind and the storm were coming.

DESCRIPTION OF THE COMING STORM OF JUDGMENT (1:4-6).

> **"He rebukes the sea and makes it dry;**
> **He dries up all the rivers.**
> **Bashan and Carmel wither;**
> **The blossoms of Lebanon wither.**
> **Mountains quake because of Him**
> **And the hills dissolve;**
> **Indeed the earth is upheaved by His presence,**
> **The world and all the inhabitants in it.**
> **Who can stand before His indignation?**
> **Who can endure the burning of His anger?**
> **His wrath is poured out like fire**
> **And the rocks are broken up by Him."** (1:4-6)

When Jesus calmed the storm on Galilee by a simple command, the disciples were stunned that anyone could command the storm to stop and it would obey. They were still learning that Jesus was a man but also fully God, who alone has the power to rebuke the sea (Mark 4:35-41). The Power of God is displayed in the poetry of Nahum. Only God can tell the sea to dry up and it obeys. He can rebuke a river or a town and make them a desert (1:4). He can dissolve the mountains and split the earth with a glance. His presence can shake the earth and everyone in it (1:5). Even the *clouds are the dust beneath His feet* (1:3).

Nineveh was the most powerful city in the most powerful kingdom on earth. People feared them, but they feared no one. That was a mistake, they should have feared the God of

Judah. God resists the proud and was about to humble them. They would become like the proud Edomites in the south who lived in caves high above the canyon floor and felt they were untouchable. But God destroyed their pride as we see in this passage in Obadiah:

> "See, I will make you small among the nations;
>   you will be utterly despised.
> The pride of your heart has deceived you,
>   you who live in the clefts of the rocks
>   and make your home on the heights,
> you who say to yourself,
>   'Who can bring me down to the ground?'
> Though you soar like the eagle
>   and make your nest among the stars,
>   from there I will bring you down,"
> declares the Lord." (Obadiah 1:2-4)

"For our God is a consuming fire" (Hebrews 12:29). No one can "endure the day of His anger" (1:6). His wrath will be like a flood of fire sweeping across the Assyrian kingdom (1:6). This was encouraging news to the people of Judah who lived in terror of the Assyrians.

GOD IS THE ONLY REFUGE IN THE COMING STORM (1:7, 8).

> The Lord is good,
> A stronghold in the day of trouble,
> And He knows those who take refuge in Him.
> But with an overflowing flood
> He will make a complete end of its site,
> And will pursue His enemies into darkness. (1:7, 8)

You have heard it said that there are two sides to every story. These two verses tell both sides. There are the people that remain true to God no matter what pressure they face to conform to an evil society. These are described as those who *"take refuge"* in God in the time of storm. God knows who they are and will be their strength when the storm of judgment arrives on the land of Judah. Their security is in the Lord and they know that He is good (1:7).

The other side of the story describes the ones that do not hide in the Lord but run to the darkness to hide. They think they are secure around others hiding in the dark of evil. God's judgment will flood over the people in their hiding places and destroy them completely. Just as God knows who are His people, His remnant, He also knows who are His enemies. This applies to all who fight against God, whether it's the wicked Ninevites or the idolaters of Judah.

These two groups of people sound very similar to a warning Jesus gave His listeners.

> **"Therefore, everyone who hears these words of Mine and acts on them, may be compared to a wise man who built his house on the rock. And the rain fell, and the floods came, and the winds blew and slammed against that house; and yet it did not fall, for it had been founded on the rock. Everyone who hears these words of Mine and does not act on them, will be like a foolish man who built his house on the sand. The rain fell, and the floods came, and the winds blew and slammed against that house; and it fell—and great was its fall." (Matthew 7:24-27)**

APPLICATION.

For any who get weary standing for the right things while others around you give up the fight, remember, God knows you. He doesn't just know your name; He knows you as part of His forever family. It is hard to stand when you feel alone, but you are never alone. He is our strength, our stronghold in the day of trouble. The day of trouble is only that, a day when compared to eternity with our Savior. Take heart, we can endure a day with the evil world breathing down our necks knowing that God is good, and we will be forever with Him. He is on our side. Don't give up.

Nineveh's doom (1:9-11).

⁹ Whatever you devise against the LORD,
He will make a complete end of it.
Distress will not rise up twice.
¹⁰ Like tangled thorns,
And like those who are drunken with their drink,
They are consumed
As stubble completely withered.
¹¹ From you has gone forth
One who plotted evil against the LORD,
A wicked counselor.

Nineveh is a sad story. They had Jonah with them 100 years earlier and even though he was a reluctant prophet, God orchestrated that visit to bring about wide-spread national repentance (Read the commentary on Jonah to see how that all happened). God spared the Ninevites then but a century later they had fallen back into their evil path. This time, judgment would not be stopped like it was before. There would not be another time for the affliction of the Assyrians to terrorize the earth because God would *"make a complete end of it"* (1:9). It seems that Assyria never missed an opportunity to miss an opportunity. They had God's favor and then lost it.

Nineveh's end would come upon them unexpectedly. They are like drunks at a party, stumbling around and laughing, not knowing the house is on fire and they will die shortly (1:10). They are like a field of dried-up thorn bushes all tangled together and a fast-moving fire comes upon the field and all are burned up (1:10). They will not be able to escape; they are too tangled up in their sins.

Verse 11 needs a short history to understand it. It tells of one who came from Nineveh, one who had an evil plot and gave bad counsel.

THE EVIL PLOT.

> "From you has gone forth
> One who plotted evil against the Lord,
> A wicked counselor." (1:11)

The king of Nineveh in the time when King Hezekiah was over Judah, was Sennacherib. He was in a military campaign that led him to Lachish, ten miles southwest of Jerusalem.

> "Several kingdoms in the Levant ceased to pay taxes to the Assyrian king Sennacherib. In retribution, he initiated a campaign to re-subjugate the rebelling kingdoms, among them the Jewish king, Hezekiah. After defeating the rebels of Ekron in Philistia, Sennacherib set out to conquer Judah and, on his way to Jerusalem, came across Lachish: the second most important of the Jewish cities." (Wiki history)

While in Lachish, Sennacherib sent his servants to Jerusalem with a message to tell the people to spread disinformation among them and discourage the people. He planned on going to Jerusalem when Lachish was taken. Here is the account in 2 Chronicles of that event:

SENNACHERIB'S PLOT AND EVIL COUNSEL.

> "With him is only an arm of flesh, but with us is the Lord our God to help us and to fight our battles." And the eople relied on the words of Hezekiah king of Judah. After this Sennacherib king of Assyria sent his servants to Jerusalem while he was besieging Lachish with all his forces with him, against Hezekiah king of Judah and against all Judah who were at Jerusalem, saying, "Thus says Sennacherib king of Assyria, 'On what are you trusting that you are remaining in Jerusalem under siege? Is not Hezekiah misleading you to give yourselves over

to die by hunger and by thirst, saying, "The Lord our God will deliver us from the hand of the king of Assyria"? Has not the same Hezekiah taken away His high places and His altars, and said to Judah and Jerusalem, "You shall worship before one altar, and on it you shall burn incense"? Do you not know what I and my fathers have done to all the peoples of the lands? Were the gods of the nations of the lands able at all to deliver their land from my hand? Who was there among all the gods of those nations which my fathers utterly destroyed who could deliver his people out of my hand, that your God should be able to deliver you from my hand? Now therefore, do not let Hezekiah deceive you or mislead you like this, and do not believe him, for no god of any nation or kingdom was able to deliver his people from my hand or from the hand of my fathers. How much less will your God deliver you from my hand?'" (2 Chronicles 32:8-15)

Nahum recounts this story as evidence against Nineveh. Nahum would have been familiar with the false counsel spread to his people from the servants of the King of Assyria, Sennacherib. We know these verses apply to Nineveh since Nahum's entire letter is against Nineveh. Remember the first words of the book of Nahum, "*The oracle of Nineveh.*" So, the text is saying, "From you, Nineveh, has come one who had a plot against the Lord and His people and used deceptive words to accomplish his purposes."

> "From you has gone forth
> One who plotted evil against the Lord,
> A wicked counselor." (1:11)

The next page will display some helpful images. The first is a sketch of the city of Lachish the year it was besieged. The second is a clay carving depicting a piece of war equipment used by the Assyrian army.

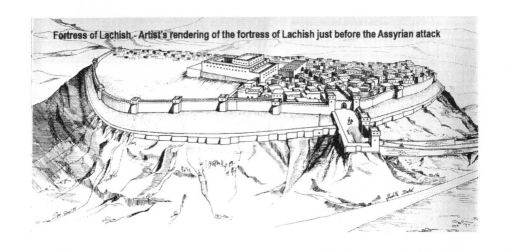

Fortress of Lachish - Artist's rendering of the fortress of Lachish just before the Assyrian attack

Assyrian siege-engine attacking the city wall of Lachish. The ascending and assaulting Assyrian military wave is overwhelming. Detail of a gypsum wall relief dating back to the reign of Sennacherib, 700-692 B.C.E. From the South-West Palace at Nineveh, Mesopotamia, modern-day Iraq, currently housed in the British Museum, London.

Encouragement for Judah that their enemy will be defeated (1:12-15).

¹² Thus says the LORD,

"Though they are at full *strength* and likewise many,
Even so, they will be cut off and pass away.
Though I have afflicted you,
I will afflict you no longer.
¹³ "So now, I will break his yoke bar from upon you,
And I will tear off your shackles."

¹⁴ The LORD has issued a command concerning you:
"Your name will no longer be perpetuated.
I will cut off idol and image
From the house of your gods.
I will prepare your grave,
For you are contemptible."

¹⁵ Behold, on the mountains the feet of him who brings good news,
Who announces peace!
Celebrate your feasts, O Judah;
Pay your vows.
For never again will the wicked one pass through you;
He is cut off completely.

Nineveh was strong and trusted in their strength. Nobody could stand against them. We saw Sennacharib mock God in the last set of verses:

> "Now therefore, do not let Hezekiah deceive you or mislead you like this, and do not believe him, for no god of any nation or kingdom was able to deliver his people from my hand or from the hand of my fathers. How much less will your God deliver you from my hand?"
> (2 Chronicles 32:15)

The Ninevites were arrogant and overconfident, they felt invincible. God was clear in His response to their pride:

> **"Thus says the Lord,**
> **'Though they are at full strength and likewise many,**
> **Even so, they will be cut off and pass away.'"** (1:12)

When kings battle other kings, they like to exploit the weaknesses of their enemies. They like to hit them when they are not at full strength. God told Nineveh He would annihilate them at full strength. They could bring the largest army in the history of the world and it didn't matter to God; they would be cut off from the land of the living. They would pass from history. God was finished with the Assyrian nation. He had given them enough warnings and even sent them a preacher. They would now be broken completely

The chains of bondage would be broken for Judah. They would never fear Nineveh again (1:13). The worst sin any person or country can make is to turn from God and worship idols. To tell God that they would rather worship a chunk of rock or a stick of wood is an unpardonable offense. Only God can save so when people say no to God's salvation, there is no other salvation. No pardon is available, the guilt and punishment remain. It is closing the door to heaven permanently. Nineveh with its numerous idols and false gods had turned from the Gospel they had heard from Jonah and now they had slammed the door of salvation. God would dig their grave and their name will pass away.

> **The Lord has issued a command concerning you:**
> **"Your name will no longer be perpetuated.**
> **I will cut off idol and image**
> **From the house of your gods.**
> **I will prepare your grave,**
> **For you are contemptible."** (1:14)

This was a two-part promise. First, Nineveh was to be removed off the earth. Today, Nineveh is only ruins, with piles of bricks and weeds growing in the desert sand.

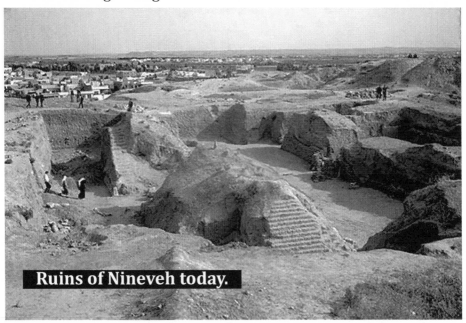

Ruins of Nineveh today.

The second part is a promise to bless Judah one day. Their name would be remembered. When Nineveh was defeated by the Babylonians, the good news was given to Judah that their arch enemy was defeated and peace was proclaimed (1:15).

> **"Behold, on the mountains the feet of him who**
> **brings good news,**
> **Who announces peace!**
> **Celebrate your feasts, O Judah;**
> **Pay your vows.**
> **For never again will the wicked one pass through you;**
> **He is cut off completely." (1:15)**

After the enemy of Judah was defeated and peace restored to the land the people could again celebrate the feasts as they had in the past. They also needed to make good on the vows and promises made. God had done His part by protecting them.

Nineveh would never again hurt Judah. This is a foretaste of the final deliverance in the future when all of the enemies of Judah will be destroyed and peace will never end.

Nahum Two

Nineveh will be attacked and defeated (2:1, 2).

¹ The one who scatters has come up against you.
Man the fortress, watch the road;
Strengthen your back, summon all *your* strength.
² For the LORD will restore the splendor of Jacob
Like the splendor of Israel,
Even though devastators have devastated them
And destroyed their vine branches.

The beginning of the assault on Nineveh by Babylon was announced. They were described as one who scatters, a destructive force that descends on their enemies like a mighty wind that scatters the crops. *"The one who scatters"* was a greater army than the Assyrian army. Only one other nation was powerful enough to take on Assyria and the city of Nineveh. History fills in the details for us. Babylon attacked Nineveh and the war was swift and devastating. After Nineveh fell, the nation soon dissolved and Babylon took over and became the greatest world power.

Even though God used the Assyrians to destroy the Northern Kingdom of Israel for its many sins, the Assyrians were also guilty of many atrocities. It was their turn to be held accountable. God reminded them that the destroyed country of His chosen people will one day be restored, unlike Nineveh, which would never rise again. God was angry with the many sins of His people but He is the God of Abraham, Isaac, and Jacob. He never forgets His promises.

The fall of Nineveh described (2:3-7).

³ The shields of his mighty men are *colored* red,
The warriors are dressed in scarlet,
The chariots are *enveloped* in flashing steel
When he is prepared *to march*,
And the cypress *spears* are brandished.
⁴ The chariots race madly in the streets,
They rush wildly in the squares,
Their appearance is like torches,
They dash to and fro like lightning flashes.
⁵ He remembers his nobles;
They stumble in their march,
They hurry to her wall,
And the mantelet is set up.
⁶ The gates of the rivers are opened
And the palace is dissolved.
⁷ It is fixed:
She is stripped, she is carried away,
And her handmaids are moaning like the sound of doves,
Beating on their breasts.

> **"This chapter is a masterpiece of ancient literature, unsurpassed for its graphic portrayal of a military assault."** (James Montgomery Boice)

Imagine being caught by surprise in a stampede of wild animals. The noise, the sounds of thundering hoofs, and the dust in your face blinding you. You would want to run, but where? They are all around you. Now, in your mind, replace those animals with war chariots of the most powerful army in the world.

> **"The shields of his mighty men are colored red,**
> **The warriors are dressed in scarlet,**
> **The chariots are enveloped in flashing steel**
> **When he is prepared to march,**
> **And the cypress spears are brandished.**
> **The chariots race madly in the streets,**
> **They rush wildly in the squares,**
> **Their appearance is like torches,**
> **They dash to and fro like lightning flashes."** (2:3, 4)

For a poetic description of an ancient battle, it reveals a lot about the Babylonian war techniques. The Medes and Babylonians were, according to historians, fond of the color red. They looked like a river of red when they entered a foreign country. It gave the impression that blood was flowing into the city. The red clothing and shields also hid the blood splatter and helped the soldiers from seeing their own blood. The color made them braver.

> **"The generals and other officers of the army were clothed**
> **in scarlet; partly to show their greatness and nobleness,**
> **and partly to strike their enemies with terror, and to hide**
> **their blood should they be wounded, and so keep up their**
> **own spirits, and not encourage their enemies"**
> (2:3, Bible Study Tools)

The sight of the disciplined Babylonian army struck terror in their enemies. They had iron on their weapons, chariots, and parts of their armor. They glistened in the sun, flashing as they attacked. They were a terrorizing force (2:3). The soldiers all carried cypress wood spears.

The chariots raced about wildly causing fear and confusion of the Ninevites. They were like torches in appearance. To the people in the town, they moved so quickly and suddenly they were like lightning flashes (2:4). It is a well-orchestrated campaign of terror that renders the enemy weaker before the slaughter. Nahum described a future event as if it was certain to happen because it was.

> **"The Medes and Chaldeans, under their respective commander or commanders, shall prepare for the siege of the city, and to make their onset and attack upon it, the chariots used by them in war, which was common in those times, would have flaming torches in them; either to guide them in the night, or to set fire to houses or tents they should meet with, or to terrify the enemy."**
> (John Gill Commentary)

The people of Nineveh became weary in the battle and were defeated.

> **"He remembers his nobles;**
> **They stumble in their march,**
> **They hurry to her wall,**
> **And the mantelet is set up.**
> **The gates of the rivers are opened**
> **And the palace is dissolved.**
> **It is fixed:**
> **She is stripped, she is carried away,**
> **And her handmaids are moaning like the sound of doves,**
> **Beating on their breasts."** (2:5-7)

The siege of Assyria lasted two years. It had to be a very tiring event for Nineveh. They were on defense the entire time. After years of strong attacks, the Assyrian warriors began to stumble to get to the wall to defend it (2:5). The final defeat came when the wall on the river side of the city was broken open and the Babylonians could enter the city. This final siege is described in a brief statement by Nahum yet it has a fascinating story that happened. Here is the sentence:

> **"The gates of the rivers are opened**
> **And the palace is dissolved."** (2:6)

The two greatest armies in the world were battling for two years and then the "gates of the rivers were opened" which brought about the end of the siege with Babylon defeating Assyria. What gates and what rivers? What happened? We need some history to fill in the rest of the story.

> **"The river wall on the Tigris (the west defense of Nineveh) was 4,530 yards long. On the north, south, and east sides, there were large moats, capable of being easily filled with water from the Khosru. Traces of dams ("gates," or sluices) for regulating the supply are still visible so that the whole city could be surrounded by a water barrier (Nahum 2:8). Besides, on the east, the weakest side, it was further protected by a lofty double rampart with a moat two hundred feet wide between its two parts, cut in the rocky ground."**

> **"The moats or canals were flooded by the Ninevites before the siege to repel the foe but later were made into a dry bed to march into the city, by the foe turning the waters into a different channel: as Cyrus did in the siege of Babylon** [Maurer].

> **"In the earlier capture of Nineveh by Arbaces the Mede, and Belesis the Babylonian, Diodorus Siculus, [1.2.80], states that there was an old prophecy that it should not be taken till the river became its enemy; so in the third year of the siege, the river by a flood broke down the walls twenty furlongs, and the king thereupon burnt himself and his palace and all his concubines and wealth together, and the enemy entered by the breach in the wall. Fire and water were doubtless the means of the second destruction here foretold, as of the first."**
> (Jamieson-Fausset-Brown Bible Commentary)

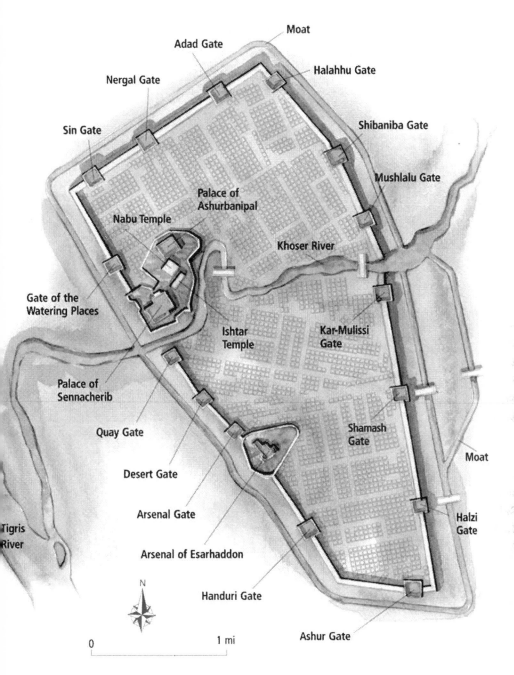

The ancient city of Nineveh - Source unknown for this map

The Babylonians dammed up the river which flowed into the city by the river gates. Then they released the water and flooded the gates which broke down the gate and a wall section. The battle ended shortly after that when the King of Nineveh locked himself in the palace and set it on fire and burned himself to death. Any that remained were taken away as slaves to Babylon. Remnants of Assyria struggled to survive after Nineveh's fall but eventually were completely conquered. The back of the Assyrian Empire had been broken.

> **"The gates of the rivers are opened
> And the palace is dissolved."** (2:6)

Reflections on the fall of Nineveh (2:8-12).

[8] Though Nineveh *was* like a pool of water throughout her days,
Now they are fleeing;
"Stop, stop,"
But no one turns back.
[9] Plunder the silver!
Plunder the gold!
For there is no limit to the treasure—
Wealth from every kind of desirable object.
[10] She is emptied! Yes, she is desolate and waste!
Hearts are melting and knees knocking!
Also anguish is in the whole body
And all their faces are grown pale!
[11] Where is the den of the lions
And the feeding place of the young lions,
Where the lion, lioness and lion's cub prowled,
With nothing to disturb *them*?
[12] The lion tore enough for his cubs,
Killed *enough* for his lionesses,
And filled his lairs with prey

174

And his dens with torn flesh.

13 "Behold, I am against you," declares the Lord of hosts. "I will burn up her chariots in smoke, a sword will devour your young lions; I will cut off your prey from the land, and no longer will the voice of your messengers be heard."

> "Though Nineveh was like a pool of water throughout her days,
> Now they are fleeing;
> 'Stop, stop,'
> But no one turns back." (2:8)

Nahum records the sorrow and lament of the fall of Nineveh before it fell. The great Tigris River supplied the Khoser River that ran through the city. The Ninevites were able to control the water around the city and store it in pools and a moat. The city was known for its beauty and tranquil pools of water. The prophet compares the city and its people to the tranquil pools before the invasion. But during and after the invasion the populace fled the city. The armies, the store merchants, everyone knew once the walls were broken down the war was over and they would be the prize of Babylon. They fled while others pled for them to stop and fight (2:8), but many of the terrified crowd did not turn back to defend the city. Once the waters were dried up by Babylon, there was a dry entrance into the city. The spoils of the city were drained out of the city. The former pools of water would become a desert. Today, it is all a desert.

Sennacherib's palace was one of the greatest and wealthiest in the world. Its waterways and rivers were legendary. The artists redition on the next page is based on what we know of the city from its ruins today.

Sennacherib's palace

> "Plunder the silver!
> Plunder the gold!
> For there is no limit to the treasure—
> Wealth from every kind of desirable object.
> She is emptied! Yes, she is desolate and waste!
> Hearts are melting and knees knocking!
> Also anguish is in the whole body
> And all their faces are grown pale!" (2:9, 10)

The city was plundered of all its vast wealth that had been accumulated from its past conquests. Nobody remained to guard its wealth after the people ran for their lives. Babylonian soldiers had no resistance when they looted the city of its wealth. The King of Nineveh, as we read earlier, barricaded himself in his palace with its wealth and burned it all down with himself and servants inside. The formerly beautiful city became a wasteland while the citizens trembled in fear (2:10). Archeologists in the years that followed have never found any gold or precious jewels in the ruins, it was all looted. Here is how an historian described what is known about the wealth of the city:

"According to Diodorus, the value of the gold taken from the temple of Bolus alone by Xerxes amounted to above 7350 Attic talents, of £21,000,000 sterling money" (Layard, 'Nineveh,' 2:416, etc.; comp. *Daniel 3:1*, where the size of the golden image or pillar, sixty cubits high and six cubits broad, shows how plentiful was gold in these countries). Bonomi: 'The riches of Nineveh are inexhaustible, her vases and precious furniture are infinite, copper constantly occurs in their weapons, and it is probably a mixture of it that was used in the materials of their tools. They had acquired the art of making glass... The well-known cylinders are sufficient proof of their skill in engraving gems. Many beautiful specimens of carving in ivory were also discovered... The condition of the ruins is highly corroborative of the sudden destruction that came upon Nineveh by fire and sword... It is evident from the ruins that both Khorsabad and Nimroud were sacked and then set on fire. Neither Botta nor Layard found any of that store of silver and gold and 'pleasant furniture' which the palaces contained; scarcely anything, even of bronze, escaped the spoiler.'"
('Nineveh and its Discoveries,' pp. 334, 336)

Destruction, Course of Empire, by Thomas Cole (1836)

Images of lions are found on the artwork of the Mesopotamian region. Assyria hunted them and used them as an image of the strength and virality of their nations. Large images of lions were found in palaces and gates of the cities. The king of the beasts became a fitting symbol of the great empires. Nahum looks through the eyes of a prophet and the coming destruction of Nineveh and asks, "Where are the lions now?"

> **"Where is the den of the lions**
> **And the feeding place of the young lions,**
> **Where the lion, lioness and lion's cub prowled,**
> **With nothing to disturb them?**
> **The lion tore enough for his cubs,**
> **Killed enough for his lionesses,**
> **And filled his lairs with prey**
> **And his dens with torn flesh."** (2:9, 10)

Assyrian lion hunt, a bas relief discovered in the ruins of Nineveh.
(British Museum)

Nahum asks, "Where is the house of the lions now?" The dens they lived in and raised their young to hunt and kill their prey. Nineveh was fallen, where is their house now where they raised their young to be mighty hunters and kill their enemies? Where are they now? Just as lions filled their lairs with what they caught, so Nineveh kept the treasures they accumulated from their victorious campaigns. Now, where are those spoils of battle? (2:9, 10)

> "'Behold, I am against you,' declares the Lord of hosts. 'I will burn up her chariots in smoke, a sword will devour your young lions; I will cut off your prey from the land, and no longer will the voice of your messengers be heard.'" (2:13)

The great warriors, the lions of Nineveh, are gone. The chariots are gone. The sound of victorious soldiers returning from battle to the sounds of cheers from the people in the fortified city of Nineveh are gone. Why? Because God said, *"Behold, I am against you."* As believers, we know that if God is for us, nobody can stand against us (Romans 8:31). But the opposite is true as well. If God is against us, nobody will stand for us. Nineveh died alone and in shame. A new lion had taken over the lair, Babylon.

The great warriors, the lions of Nineveh, are gone.

Nahum Three
NAHUM MOCKS AND CELEBRATES THE FALL OF ASSYRIA

INTRODUCTION TO CHAPTER THREE.

This chapter is a taunt, a mockery of the soon-to-fall city of Nineveh. People of all generations have used this form of sarcastic mockery. Zephaniah was another prophet used by God to predict judgment against Nineveh. Here is a taunt he gave of the beautiful city that thought she was invincible.

> **"This is the exultant city**
> **Which dwells securely,**
> **Who says in her heart,**
> **'I am, and there is no one besides me.'**
> **How she has become a desolation,**
> **A resting place for beasts!**
> **Everyone who passes by her will hiss**
> **And wave his hand in contempt."** (Zephaniah 2:15)

Isaiah, the prophet, told the people of Judah that they would one day take up a taunt against the King of Babylon, who like Assyria, mocked God and even thought he could be equal with God. The words the King of Babylon quoted came from another ruler, Satan, who first tried them and was cast out of God's presence.

> **"But you said in your heart,**
> **'I will ascend to heaven;**
> **I will raise my throne above the stars of God,**
> **And I will sit on the mount of assembly**
> **In the recesses of the north.**
> **I will ascend above the heights of the clouds;**

I will make myself like the Most High.'
Nevertheless you will be thrust down to Sheol,
To the recesses of the pit.
Those who see you will gaze at you,
They will ponder over you, saying,
'Is this the man who made the earth tremble,
Who shook kingdoms.'" (Isaiah 14:13-16)

Nahum continued the tradition of taunting the nations that mocked God and faced the judgment of God. Nineveh would be beaten down and humiliated. And one day the same fate would come to Babylon.

Nineveh's complete ruin and humiliation (3:1-7).

¹ Woe to the bloody city, completely full of lies *and* pillage;
Her prey never departs.
² The noise of the whip,
The noise of the rattling of the wheel,
Galloping horses
And bounding chariots!
³ Horsemen charging,
Swords flashing, spears gleaming,
Many slain, a mass of corpses,
And countless dead bodies—
They stumble over the dead bodies!
⁴ *All* because of the many harlotries of the harlot,
The charming one, the mistress of sorceries,
Who sells nations by her harlotries
And families by her sorceries.
⁵ "Behold, I am against you," declares the LORD of hosts;
"And I will lift up your skirts over your face,
And show to the nations your nakedness

And to the kingdoms your disgrace.
⁶"I will throw filth on you
And make you vile,
And set you up as a spectacle.
⁷"And it will come about that all who see you
Will shrink from you and say,
'Nineveh is devastated!
Who will grieve for her?'
Where will I seek comforters for you?"

Nahum begins with a description of the carnage of the siege of Nineveh. Everything would be destroyed, everything! All the citizens would be enslaved who stayed in the city. The city was evil, filled with constant bloodshed, lies, and thefts. It was never without victims of its crimes.

> **"Woe to the bloody city, completely full of lies and pillage; Her prey never departs."** (3:1)

Historians have described the bloodshed and cruelty of the Ninevites. The Ninevites claimed in their writings to have burned 3,000 prisoners to death, skinned many alive, beheaded many, and formed pillars from the skulls and numerous other atrocities. It was a busy city with the sound of chariots and whips heard all the time. Soldiers with their swords and spears were busy executing prisoners. Now, it has come full circle. Nineveh is about to reap as they have sown. This passage continues with the description of the siege of the city and the slaughter of the Ninevites. Nineveh was brutal and now a people more brutal is treating them the way they treated others. Masses of corpses are piled in the streets, so much that people are stumbling over the dead to escape. It is a time of terror for the Ninevites. Those who had abused their prisoners and mocked them will now be the ones abused and mocked. The horror of how they treated others has now come back to terrorize them. We are reminded of a New Testament warning, *"Do not be deceived, God is not mocked; for whatever a person sows, this he will also reap."* (Galatians 6:7)

> **"The noise of the whip,**
> **The noise of the rattling of the wheel,**
> **Galloping horses**
> **And bounding chariots!**
> **Horsemen charging,**
> **Swords flashing, spears gleaming,**
> **Many slain, a mass of corpses,**
> **And countless dead bodies—**
> **They stumble over the dead bodies!"** (3:2, 3)

Erich Lessing/Art Resource, NY

Nahum then described the wickedness of Nineveh. The sins listed include immorality which was connected with temple prostitution and also with the dark arts of sorcery and witchcraft. They were also guilty of leading other nations into these despicable sins

> "All because of the many harlotries of the harlot,
> The charming one, the mistress of sorceries,
> Who sells nations by her harlotries
> And families by her sorceries." (3:4)

Nineveh was a center of magic, incantations, and spells. They recorded these on clay tablets which can be found in museums today.

These clay tablets record a prophecy about a battle Assyria was facing. Magicians received the prophecy by use of sorcery using a liver from a sacrificial sheep. (Displayed in the Metropolitan Museum)

"During the first millennium B.C., expert practitioners of magic performed rituals and practiced other facets of magic production in private and public contexts. Our knowledge of these practices comes from extensive cuneiform records that preserve descriptions of these specialists, their technical knowledge, the spells they recited, the medicinal substances they made, and the knowledge necessary to interpret signs in the natural world. Under the direction of the Assyrian kings, many of these spells and practices became standardized, and texts were formalized into several canonical series referred to as 'handbooks,' many of which were recovered from the famous Library of Ashurbanipal in Nineveh, and from the city of Sippar, one of the great Mesopotamian centers of learning." (The Metropolitan Museum, New York City)

These practices were warned about very clearly by God during the times of Moses.

"When you enter the land which the Lord your God gives you, you shall not learn to imitate the detestable things of those nations. There shall not be found among you anyone who makes his son or his daughter pass through the fire, one who uses divination, one who practices witchcraft, or one who interprets omens, or a sorcerer, or one who casts a spell, or a medium, or a spiritist, or one who calls up the dead. For whoever does these things is detestable to the Lord; and because of these detestable things the Lord your God will drive them out before you."
(Deuteronomy 18:9-12)

What would God do to a people that practiced satanic rituals and sacrifices and led others to the dark side?

"'Behold, I am against you,' declares the Lord of hosts;
'And I will lift up your skirts over your face,
And show to the nations your nakedness
And to the kingdoms your disgrace.
I will throw filth on you
And make you vile,
And set you up as a spectacle.

And it will come about that all who see you
Will shrink from you and say,
"Nineveh is devastated!
Who will grieve for her?'
Where will I seek comforters for you?"'" (3:5-7)

God responded with *"I am against you."* All of Nineveh's magicians, astrologers, spells, and sacrifices were of no value or help. Nineveh had a great turning to God one hundred years earlier when Jonah preached. They understood that God is the only King and He does not tolerate any other gods before Him. They even had Jonah's tomb in Nineveh as a memorial of that great event. However, they returned to their sin fulfilling Proverbs 26:11, *"Like a dog that returns to its vomit is a fool who repeats his folly."* First they turned back to God and then later they turned their back on God. God uses terminology that was normally used for immoral women who were publically displayed and humiliated. God will expose their sins, *"lift up their skirts"* (3:5, 6).

> **"They put such women in the pillory as a gazing-stock;**
> **and then, children and others threw mud, dirt, and filth of**
> **all kinds at them."** (Adam Clarke Commentary)

The humiliation will be so great that all who see Nineveh exposed and covered with her filth will pull away from her. None will be found to comfort her in her shame. For Nineveh, her sins will be shouted from the housetops.

> **"And it will come about that all who see you**
> **Will shrink from you and say,**
> **'Nineveh is devastated!**
> **Who will grieve for her?'**
> **Where will I seek comforters for you?"** (3:7)

"The ancient Greek historian Diodorus Siculus wrote of the destruction of Nineveh: "So great was the multitude of the slain that the flowing stream, mingled with their blood, changed its color for a considerable distance... They plundered the spoil of the city, a quantity beyond counting." (James Montgomery Boice)

The lessons of Nineveh are for all of us. There is nothing hidden in the sight of God. Everything will be revealed in His time.

"Accordingly, whatever you have said in the dark will be heard in the light, and what you have whispered in the inner rooms will be proclaimed upon the housetops." (Luke 12:3)

What Nineveh did to Egypt would one day happen to Nineveh (3:8-11).

⁸ Are you better than No-amon,
Which was situated by the waters of the Nile,
With water surrounding her,
Whose rampart *was* the sea,
Whose wall *consisted* of the sea?
⁹ Ethiopia was *her* might,
And Egypt too, without limits.
Put and Lubim were among her helpers.
¹⁰ Yet she became an exile,
She went into captivity;
Also her small children were dashed to pieces
At the head of every street;
They cast lots for her honorable men,
And all her great men were bound with fetters.
¹¹ You too will become drunk,
You will be hidden.
You too will search for a refuge from the enemy.

God now asks Nineveh a question:

> **"Are you better than No-amon,**
> **Which was situated by the waters of the Nile?"** (3:8)

As we will see, the point of this question was to show the Ninevites and all of Assyria that just as the Egyptian city of No-amon was destroyed because of their idolatry and wickedness, so Nineveh would also be destroyed. They were no better than the city they had destroyed. For the same reasons God used the Assyrians to destroy No-amon, God would use the Babylonians to destroy Assyria. But before we leave these verses, there are so many fascinating parts to this story. Let's briefly look at the history behind this event.

What happened is an example of the Golden Rule (Matthew 7:12). We should treat others the way we would like to be treated. Usually, we read that Rule in a positive way. We should treat others well if we want to be treated well. The opposite is true as well. If we treat others poorly, are we not saying we want to be treated in the same way? We have just seen some of the horrible practices of the Ninevites. They were brutal in how they invaded, tortured, and killed their enemies. It should not be surprising to think they would end up being treated the same way in the end. Nahum in these verses (3:8-11) is saying exactly that.

The example given is that of a city in Egypt named No-amon which was on the Nile river. No-amon is the Hebrew word for the city of Thebes, the capital city of Upper Egypt. The Prophet Jeremiah provides us some insight into this city.

> **"The LORD Almighty, the God of Israel, says: "I am about to**
> **bring punishment on Amon, god of Thebes, on Pharaoh,**
> **on Egypt and her gods and her kings, and on those who**
> **rely on Pharaoh."** (Jeremiah 46:25, NIV)

No-Amon (Thebes) was an important city, named after one of the gods of Egypt. Along with Jeremiah, Ezekiel also predicted its destruction (Ezekiel 30:14). No-amon was a stronghold of Egypt but God decreed it would be destroyed because of its wickedness. The city was named after the god Amon, the city's name means "the house of Amon." This was the same sun god "Ra" that Moses dealt with when God Almighty sent Egypt into darkness, removing the sun for three days (Exodus 10). The plagues on Egypt were God's response to the false deities of Egypt. Ra, the sun god, was shown to Egypt to be no match for the One true God. This false god of Egypt was also called Amun-Ra. In Greek mythology, the god was identified as Zeus.

> "As the chief deity of the Egyptian Empire, Amun-Ra also came to be worshipped outside Egypt, according to the testimony of ancient Greek historiographers in Libya and Nubia. As Zeus Ammon, he came to be identified with Zeus in Greece." (Wiki encyclopedia)

Here is one final commentary that adds some additional information to the story and explains the reason for verses 8-11. When God decreed the end of the wicked city of Thebes, He used the Assyrians as the executioner. God, in the same way, used Assyria to execute judgment on His people, Israel, for their sins, most notably idolatry. The Assyrians not only brought about God's judgment on No-amon, but they did it with brutality as you will see in the following description:

> "If No-Amon has fallen, the city of the hundred gates, the metropolis of the Pharaohs, the conqueror whose countless captives reared the pyramids, why shall Nineveh stand? If Nineveh is protected by rivers—the Tigris and the Khausser—had not Thebes a rampart in the Nile, that "sea" of waters, and its numerous canals? If Nineveh relies on subordinate or friendly states—Mesopotamia, Babylonia, Syria—had not Thebes all the resources of

Africa—Ethiopia in the south, Egypt in the north, her Libyan allies, Put and the Lubim, in the north-west? Yet what was the fate of No Amon? Her youth carried off in the slave-gangs of Assyria; her infants dashed to pieces at the street-corner (2Kings 8:12), as unprofitable to the captor; her senators reserved to grace a triumph, and assigned to the Assyrian generals by lot."
(Obadiah 1:11, Ellicott's commentary)

This gives us a picture of what was happening. God used the Assyrian empire to bring about the destruction of the city of Thebes, the capital city of northern Egypt. Thebes, known as the "House of the sun god Amon", was a center of worship of the false gods of Egypt. Ra-amun is equated to Baal in Israel, an abomination to the True and Living God. The question God asks of Nineveh is: "What makes you think you are any better than Egypt?" You are just as bad as they were. You are brutal. You worship false gods. You are just as guilty. You too will be destroyed just as you destroyed them. Her alliances did not save her and yours won't save you (3:9). Just as you took her into captivity and smashed the children into pieces, so it will happen to you (3:10). You bound her mighty men and gambled among yourselves for them and that is going to happen to you (3:10). They tried to find help, a hiding place but none could be found. That will also soon be your story as well.

Every security Nineveh trusted in would fail them. (3:12-15).

¹² All your fortifications are fig trees with ripe fruit—
When shaken, they fall into the eater's mouth.
¹³ Behold, your people are women in your midst!
The gates of your land are opened wide to your enemies;

Fire consumes your gate bars.
¹⁴ Draw for yourself water for the siege!
Strengthen your fortifications!
Go into the clay and tread the mortar!
Take hold of the brick mold!
¹⁵ There fire will consume you,
The sword will cut you down;
It will consume you as the locust *does*.
Multiply yourself like the creeping locust,
Multiply yourself like the swarming locust.

Nineveh was a proud city. It had strong walls they felt were impenetrable. Nahum reminded them that no barrier was safe when God raises the enemy to defeat them. He tells them that their great fortifications would be like fragile fig trees that receive a shaking causing all the fruit to dislodge and fall into their enemy's mouth (3:12). Nahum next described the city that trusted in its mighty men, the soldiers of the powerful army, being like a group of women to take on the invading army. Not just women, but women who leave the gates unguarded and flee. The enemy will enter like a flood and the gates will be burned down (3:13). Nahum's point was the city was unprepared for the invasion that was coming.

The city was warned to get enough water to set aside for the battle. Walls and gates required additional strengthening so they needed to make more bricks to finish the job (3:14). At best it will only delay the inevitable, Nineveh would not survive the attack. Fire will burn it down and people will be killed with the sword. The invasion will be so great it will be like a swarm of locusts destroying the crops (3:15).

The principle is clear: nothing that man makes, no matter how great, will last forever. This is especially true when God is not favorable to the project.

"Unless the Lord builds the house,
They labor in vain who build it;
Unless the Lord guards the city,
The watchman keeps awake in vain." (Psalm 127:1)

The leaders of Nineveh had failed them. (3:16-19).

16 You have increased your traders more than the stars of heaven—
The creeping locust strips and flies away.
17 Your guardsmen are like the swarming locust.
Your marshals are like hordes of grasshoppers
Settling in the stone walls on a cold day.
The sun rises and they flee,
And the place where they are is not known.
18 Your shepherds are sleeping, O king of Assyria;
Your nobles are lying down.
Your people are scattered on the mountains
And there is no one to regather *them*.
19 There is no relief for your breakdown,
Your wound is incurable.
All who hear about you
Will clap *their* hands over you,
For on whom has not your evil passed continually?

Nahum's taunt continues. He sarcastically commends Nineveh for the way they continued to expand their merchants, guards, commanders, army generals, local leaders, and nobility. With all that growth, things must be healthy, right? Not so. Nineveh may have had more merchants than the stars of heaven but they were bankrupt in their souls and soon their stalls would be empty. There would be nothing left to sell. They had more guards than a swarm of locusts but they would flee when the trials come (3:17). What good are guards if they don't stick around? What good are all the shepherds if they don't watch the flocks? They would be asleep when the wolves come (3:18). Your leaders and nobles would flee to the mountains like rats abandoning a sinking ship (3:18). The complete society of Nineveh was going to come crashing down. They had a fatal wound that could not be healed, an incurable disease. Evil infected the city and nation (3:19). There was great rejoicing at the fall of Nineveh (3:19).

When a great plague has infected a population there is no relief. The graves will be all that is left as a reminder that a great city once stood at that site. Nineveh was one of the greatest cities of the ancient world but they could not stop the judgment of God. Their sins against God and man brought about the end of their season of power. Today, a few signs in the city of Mosul, Iraq, direct you to the field of ruins and weeds growing in the desert sand. The entire area is like a large gravestone with the words, "This is all that remains of the once-great city that rejected God and paid the awful price."

An Assyrian winged human-headed lion from Nimrud NW Palace (British Museum)